M RAVI

HUNG AT DAWN

 ORION BOOKS

Copyright 2005

Graphics and Print Management by R G BEE Publications.

Edited and researched by Renard Alban Laine.

Photos by Jack Sim.

All Rights reserved. Portions copyright.

First Printing, Dec 2005 in Singapore.

First Published in Singapore in 2005 by :

M. Ravi

20 Havelock Road,

#02-10, Central Square,

Singapore 059765.

Tel: 6428 8370

Fax: 6428 8371

Email: mravilaw@gmail.com

ISBN: 981-05-4848-6

Forward

"Hung At Dawn" provides a vivid insight into the dehumanising process that leads to the state killing of death row prisoners in Singapore. Detailing the impact on those drawn into the process - including the condemned, their relatives, lawyers, police, judges and executioners - the narrative asks the uncomfortable question as to why Singapore has the highest per capita execution rate in the world.

In describing frantic legal efforts to prevent a hanging, the reader is forced to confront the reality that, while no judicial system is immune from error, the taking of a prisoner's life is final and irrevocable. The appalling prospect of the innocent being led to their death is driven home, when, in answer to a question during a last-minute appeal whether an innocent man could be hanged for procedural reasons, the Chief Justice replied "Yes".

Singaporeans opposed to capital punishment have tried for many years to prompt greater public debate on the issue, and this book is an important contribution to that effort. Many hope the day when Singapore recognises executions as a violation of human rights without any unique deterrent effect against crime, and so joins the world-wide trend towards abolition of the death penalty, may have come a small step closer.

Timothy Parritt, Amnesty International

This book would not have been possible

without the encouragement and

assistance of many people.

I would especially like to thank

the following individuals:

Lucy Davis

Violet Netto

Linda Ruck

Seelan

This book is in memory of my late Mother

PAPA

I wish to express my profound gratitude to my Divine Mother

PAPA now in Her Formless Form.

I am convinced that She oversees everything I do and guides me along the chosen path;

AND

to all the mothers who have lost their beloved children at the merciless hands of state murderers all over the world;

AND

I would also like to thank those few people who stood alongside me in the struggle for Vignes' life, and also the growing number of Singaporeans dedicating themselves to the fight to abolish the death penalty in Singapore as exemplified by the campaigns for Shanmugam Murugesu and Nguyen Tuong Van.

CONTENTS

CHAPTERS

Prologue

THE LAST GRASP

The early morning sun streamed along the edges of his building, but Vignes Mourthi's room was spared the brash light that would otherwise have jolted him awake. Vignes roused himself and finally pulled himself out of bed that Thursday morning. He hadn't gotten much sleep really.. he had been tossing and turning most of the night. He made his way to the toilet bowl, relieved himself, then shuffled over to the metal sheeting he used as a mirror. He brushed back his thick hair and closely regarded his appearance. He knew he needed to make the best impression he could that day. He didn't have to worry about what he should wear though. That matter had already been decided for him.

Vignes started walking around the narrow confines of his room, wondering what else he could do over the next several hours to make the time go by less slowly. Or should he just try to savour each moment of that time?

This Thursday was, after all, unlike any other day he had ever experienced. Because the simple fact was that unless his lawyer was successful at pulling off a feat that had almost no chance of success, this would be Vignes' last full day alive.

Vignes' lawyer, R. Martin, had also started his day earlier than usual that crucial Thursday. He knew that this was indeed a last-ditch effort and he had to pull out every weapon in his arsenal to swing the case his way. And even then, it might not be enough.

Martin was actually the fourth defence lawyer handling this case. In fact, he had only been on the case for three weeks. Since then, he had been working overtime-plus on the matter, trying to marshal any possible and feasible argument that could save his client's life, even at this dramatically late date.

Many might even have adjudged Martin's cause as beyond hopeless at this late hour, less than 24 hours before Vignes' scheduled execution. Yet, all he was striving to do at this point was to get a stay of execution so that he could file a later appeal for a new trial. In many countries, this would have been a much easier task. But this was Singapore, where judicial rules are stringent, and the state's justice does not like to tarry, just because something new could turn up.

Martin put the final finishing touches on his preparations, peeked at his watch and grimaced. He would have supporters with him there in the courtroom, and a great many more behind him. The question was, would any of this be enough to influence the court, not usually inclined to grant stays at any time, certainly not this late in the process. It was time for him to leave for Singapore's Supreme Court, just a short ride from his office.

Back in his cell, Vignes Mourthi had finished dressing, and sat back on his mattress. There were hundreds of thoughts and images racing through his mind, but he tried to concentrate on just the most important of them. Had there been a window in his cell, he might have gazed out that window and tried to give his imagination some wider scope. But death row inmates in Singapore are kept in the bowels of the prison, with no direct connection to the natural world they've been removed from. If this fact had once bothered him considerably, it was of no concern now. He had other matters to occupy himself with.

Actually, Vignes Mourthi had nothing more to do but wait for his 2 p.m.

hearing. He had no other plans to make for the day. And if this appeal, too, failed, he wouldn't have to plan much further ahead than the next day either. Because if Mr. Martin's skills didn't pull off a near miracle, Vignes would be hanged early the next morning in another part of this prison that had served as his home for most of the last two years.

Chapter 1

APPLYING THE STING

There is no agony like bearing an untold story inside of you.

- Maya Angelou

Vignes Mourthi's troubled journey to this point had all begun just over two years before, on 20 September 2001. Or maybe it was that fateful evening of 19 September. A native of Ipoh in Malaysia, Vignes was the son of an ethnic Indian couple who together ran a small coffee stall back in Ipoh.

Many immigrants from India, as well as first-generation and second-generation Indians in that part of Malaysia, worked in the local mines or on one of the large rubber plantations not far from the main town. Vignes' parents had both worked on a rubber plantation when they were young; it was there, in fact, that they had met. After they married, they managed, with the help of family, to scrape together enough money to move off the plantations and open the small coffee shop. They did not make much money from the stall, barely enough to support themselves and a family of four children.

Seeing far better job opportunities in Johor and Singapore, the land of milk and honey just across the causeway from Johor, 18-year-old Vignes headed south in 1999.

Singapore is, indeed, a land of milk and honey for many Malaysians. Only 1/500th the size of Malaysia, it boasts a per capita GDP over two-and-a-half times greater than that of its northern neighbour. Singapore is renowned for its bustling economy and its hard-working labour force. But many in that labour force aren't Singaporeans. In fact, the Singapore economy would take a rapid plunge if it suddenly had to make do without the thousands of foreign workers contributing to that impressive GDP.

Pay scales in Singapore are, almost across the board, higher than in Malaysia - sometimes significantly so. This is the handsome bait that lures Malaysians of all income levels down south of the Causeway joining the two Southeast Asian "Little Tigers".

Of course, prices for most things are also higher in Singapore than in Malaysia. This is what keeps the long queues of autos and mini-vans waiting to cross the checkpoint from Singapore into Malaysia almost every Saturday and Sunday. These vehicles are mostly filled with Singaporeans on their weekly shopping run, hoping to stock up on the profusion of bargains waiting in shops and malls across the Causeway.

There is a kind of vehicular ebb and flow at the Singapore-Malaysia checkpoints, especially the main one at Woodlands. On the weekends, you see the northbound lanes clogged with all of those autos and mini-vans filled with well-to-do Singaporeans making shopping runs to pick up enticing buys in Malaysia. On the weekdays, and to a lesser extent on Saturdays and Sundays as well, you'll find the southbound lanes filled with beaten-up trucks and vans ferrying low-cost Malaysian workers heading off to their southern neighbour where even their skimpy wages are more attractive than what they can earn at those same low-skilled jobs back home.

Despite Singapore's higher cost of living, on balance it's still better, financially at least, to earn your living there in the Lion City (Singapore's nickname). The best strategy, however, is to work in Singapore and live in Malaysia, travelling five, six, sometimes even seven days a week back and forth, rain or punishing sun, across the Causeway. This, in fact, is what young Vignes Mourthi had been doing for close to five years.

In September 2001, Vignes was working at Exel, a multinational supply chain management firm specialising in contract logistics and freight management. Vignes, or Vicky, as he was commonly known to close friends and family, was pulling in about $1,400 Singapore a month as a machine operator-packer. This would be considered a rather modest income by Singaporean standards, but Vignes' father claimed that his son sent back two-thirds of his salary every month to his parents.

Truth is, for someone from his background, that $1,400 income was not bad at all. Never a very good student, Mourthi had only made it to secondary school. There, he failed most of his O levels, and then decided to leave school and seek work. He trained as a machine operator and took a string of moderately low-paying jobs before finding employment in Singapore. It was the best job he had held in his entire life. And, by most accounts, he took advantage of the opportunity: he worked long hours, worked hard and never let his employers hear any complaints. Just the kind of foreign worker they wanted.

But he was not indestructible.. or fortune's favourite child. On 15 September 2001, Vignes had a minor accident while riding his motorcycle back to Malaysia at the end of a long week's work. He was able to get up quickly from the spill, but did suffer light injuries to his leg which earned him medical leave through September 19. It also cost him the use of his motorcycle, which sorely needed repairs. This accident proved to be just the start of a week of spiralling misfortunes for Vignes Mourthi.

Towards the end of that week, Vignes was preparing to return to his work at Exel the next day. On the evening of 19 September, Vignes was attending services at a Hindu temple near his home when an old family friend, Moorthy Angappan, dropped by at Vignes' house around 8:30pm. Informed that

Vignes was at the temple with his wife, Moorthy asked if he could wait there until the couple returned as he had something he really needed to discuss with his young friend. Vignes' family (his two sisters and uncle were also present at the time) cordially invited Moorthy to make himself at home. This was a courtesy natural and expected, as Moorthy had been close to the family for a number of years.

Moorthy only had to wait about half an hour for Vignes to return from the temple. After exchanging Tamil greetings, the two men sat down to discuss what seemed to be a small matter: Moorthy asked Vignes if he could bring a small packet with him to Singapore when he went to work the next day, then drop off this packet to an associate of Moorthy's, a fellow identified only as Tahir. Tahir would even come out to meet Vignes at Changi, that northeast corner of Singapore near where the young machine operator worked. Oh yes: Moorthy also mentioned that Tahir would be turning something over to Vignes when they met: an envelope full of money.

Moorthy even told Vignes how much he would be getting from this Tahir fellow - 8,000 Singapore dollars, a fair amount of cash for people in their social strata. (Remember that Vignes himself only earned $1,400 a month at his six-day-a-week job.) The younger man later explained that he had the impression this sum was either a loan for some poultry business Moorthy was planning to start up or a repayment of a debt that Tahir owed to Moorthy.

Vignes readily agreed to do his family friend this favour, which hardly seemed much of a burden at the time. Moorthy thanked him, then added he would return a little later with the package he needed turned over to Tahir.

'A little later' proved to be much later than Vignes had expected. It wasn't until around 2 a.m. that Moorthy returned and started knocking on the door of his friend's house. The knocking woke up Vignes' wife, who then roused her husband. Vignes trundled out to the front door, let Moorthy in and took the package from this late-night visitor. The package actually turned out to be two plastic bags: one white with another, smaller red bag stuffed inside. The red bag contained the item to be delivered to Tahir. When a still woozy Vignes inquired what the red bag contained, he was told it was just incense stones, a coarsely ground material frequently used in Hindu ceremonies. Moorthy Angappan had once owned a company that dealt in this religious commodity, so his explanation would have made sense - especially to someone only half-awake.

Moorthy also handed his young friend a slip of paper with Tahir's mobile phone number on it. He should, he was told, call Tahir sometime that morning and arrange a pick-up time and point.

Still rather groggy and needing to get up again in just a few hours, Vignes quickly wrapped up this business, saw his friend out and then dropped the plastic bag on a small coffee table in the hallway of his home before returning to bed.

Johor Bahru was still wrapped in dark when Vignes mounted the motorcycle of a friend at 5:15 am the morning of September 20. He was riding pillion with this friend, named Jayacelan, as his own bike was still damaged from the accident five days earlier. At that early hour, the traffic at the checkpoint into Singapore was not too heavy, so the two men made good time. Jayacelan, who worked at the same Singapore firm but in another department, dropped Vignes off at his place of work sometime between 6:15 and 6:30am.

Around 8 a.m., Vignes managed a break and called Tahir at the number written down on the slip of paper given him the night before. Tahir said he would try to borrow a car and drive all the way over to Vignes' place of work to pick up the delivery. Nearly an hour later, Vignes called Moorthy to inform him that he had tentatively arranged pick-up with this Tahir.

However, after a short time back at work, Vignes' leg injury started to bother him again. The pain only increased as he tried to concentrate on his duties. Finally, he managed to wrangle an additional half-day's leave from his supervisor and decided to head home as soon as he could. But first, he had to take care of that business with Tahir. The big question was, how to get that packet to him.

Vicky then called Moorthy one more time and asked if he himself could come down and see to the delivery as his pain made it imperative that Vignes get back home as soon as possible. Moorthy replied that he couldn't come down just yet, as he was waiting for an important phone call from a customer. If Vignes could just bear with his pain a little longer, hand the packet over to Tahir, then wait for him, Moorthy would arrange to borrow a motorcycle and be down shortly to pick up his young friend and give him a ride back to Johor. Reluctantly, Vignes agreed.

Within a short time, however, Vignes himself had borrowed a motorcycle from a colleague at Exel, Vayapuri, who also happened to be both a relative and a good friend of his. He quickly called Tahir to tell him of his change of schedule and arranged to drop off the bags at the An Nur mosque in Woodlands, a short distance from the border checkpoint, in about 30 to 45 minutes.

But Vignes' streak of bad luck continued on his ride over to An Nur. The motorcycle he had borrowed suffered a punctured tire, forcing the young man to pull over and park it on the side of a road. Fortunately, he quickly managed to hitch a ride from another bikie.

When Vignes finally arrived at the mosque, no one fitting Tahir's description was to be seen. He again rang up Tahir on his mobile phone, to see what the problem was. This time, the phone was answered by a man who identified himself as 'Segar'. Some other matter had come up for Tahir apparently; 'Segar' would be the one coming around directly to pick up the package. He said that he'd arrive in a silver-car bearing the license plate 9073, so Vignes should just keep an eye out for this vehicle. He estimated it would take him about 10 to 15 minutes to reach the mosque from where he was.

Vignes had in the meantime phoned his friend Moorthy back in Johor and asked him to shoot down to Woodlands and make the delivery to Tahir himself. This was supposedly because of the increasing pain he was experiencing. Moorthy told Vignes to stay put, make the exchange with Tahir, and that he would be along very shortly to pick his injured friend up and transport him back to his home.

A short time later, a silver car with license plate 9073 pulled up, and a long-haired Indian man stepped out. Vignes happened to notice that the driver of the vehicle was a Chinese fellow. The long-haired Indian gentleman introduced himself as Segar and asked Vignes if he was, in fact, Vignes. Vignes said he was, then pulled the red plastic bag out of his riding helmet. But before handing the bag over, he asked Segar about the money he was supposed to receive from Tahir. The latter nodded, then pulled out a thick wad of notes and handed this over to Vignes. Vignes checked just briefly to see if it was the $8,000 he had been told about and Segar assured him it was.

The young man then handed over the red bag to Segar. The bag now in his possession, Segar smiled and gave Vignes a thumbs-up. Despite the pains in his leg, Vignes himself was rather heartened by this thumbs-up sign, taking it as an indication of satisfaction from Segar. Vignes was also thinking that he had carried out this delivery effectively, despite all the glitches he had encountered that day.

But that thumbs-up was not just a sign of customer satisfaction from Segar. It was primarily a signal to eight of his associates, who were lying in wait at various points around the mosque. This eight-man squad rushed up; two of them seized Vignes as he started to move away. And from that moment on, his life would never be the same again.

'Segar' was actually Sergeant S. Rajkumar from Singapore's Central Narcotics Bureau (CNB), and the eight men who had surrounded and seized Vignes, as well as the Chinese driver of the silver car, were also CNB agents. Vignes Mourthi had become the victim of a deftly orchestrated police sting. When the agents opened the red bag and peered inside, they were satisfied that they had received just what they had been expecting - heroin. However, as they later determined, it was not entirely what they had expected: informed that they would be purchasing one kilo of heroin, they only got 27.65 grams. That's one of the hazards of buying illicit drugs - you can't always rely on the honesty of your dealer.

But was Vignes Mourthi actually a dealer - or just an unwitting dupe? The wrangling over this question would develop into a legal tug-of-war that would go on for most of the next two years. And Vignes Mourthi's very life hung in the balance of what the correct answer was. Or the answer that the authorities ultimately chose to believe. Incredibly, the whole case would ultimately turn on a single word, and whether that word was actually uttered or not.

Let's reel this back for a moment. The above is Vignes' own account of those fateful two days in September 2001. Sgt. Rajkumar had a rather different version. And Moorthy Angappan, the family friend then heading into Woodlands to meet up with Vignes, had an even more different version.

Moorthy, whose lawyer would later describe him as a very helpful person, had, as promised, travelled down to Singapore on a borrowed motorcycle to fetch the injured Vignes. He was waiting in the vicinity of a fruit shop on Woodlands Centre Road, almost within sight of the An Nur mosque when Vignes called him on one of the CNB agents' phones to find out where they should meet. Moorthy told his young friend where he was. A short time later, two cars drove up to a spot not far from the fruit shop where Moorthy was waiting.

Vignes was in one of those cars. He peered out the window, then identified one man standing there wearing a grey shirt as his "brother" (a term of affection more than blood relation). The head of the sting operation, ASP Krishnan, and another CNB officer then approached Moorthy. They identified themselves as CNB agents and asked Moorthy what he was doing lingering near the fruit shop. He replied that he was simply waiting for a friend. When they asked him the name of this friend, Moorthy refused to answer. He was then arrested by the two CNB agents as part of that drug transaction they had just intercepted. Life had just taken a vicious spin downwards for Moorthy as well.

As he was being hauled off, Moorthy anxiously repeated, "What happened, what happened?" and asked why he was being arrested. The agents were not in a very talkative mood, however; they simply pushed Moorthy into a second car, then sped him off to the Clementi Police Station in western Singapore. This was the same place they had just taken Vignes Moorthy - his accomplice, dupe or false accuser. The police then set out to untangle the many ragged threads of this case. It would not be an easy task.

Vignes had actually 'flipped' on the second accused man almost immediately. Soon after Vignes was placed in the back of the police car, Sgt. Rajkumar started to question the suspect, who insisted that he had been given the fateful packet by his anneh (Tamil for 'elder brother') and that this brother was now nearby, waiting to collect the ill-gotten money from him. During the initial stage of questioning at the Clementi station (which began around 2 p.m. on the day of the arrest), Vignes again insisted that he had received the stuff from Moorthy, whom he proceeded to identify from a passport photo the police showed him.

That evening, Vignes was again questioned by the police. He repeated his charge that Moorthy had given him the drugs, asked him to pass the packet along to Tahir and to collect the $8,000 from this shadowy figure. He further insisted, "I do not know the stuff was heroin. Moorthy told me the stuff were stones. I have not seen heroin before. When I was arrested, then only I knew it was some sort of drugs."

(Vignes would later testify that he also had no idea what that large amount of money was for. He maintained that he "did not want to ask" why Moorthy would be getting $8,000 from Tahir. In Vignes' culture, it could be seen as a sign of disrespect for him to probe into such a matter with his anneh - almost like asking about his intimate relations with his wife.)

Vignes repeated his assertions about Moorthy's key involvement in subsequent interrogations on the 24th, 26th and 27th of September. As Vignes and his attorney later argued, the young man from northern Malaysia had no qualms about implicating this old family friend, as Moorthy had lied to him, tricked him into being his 'mule' and set him up for a possible death sentence. Any bonds of loyalty between them had been totally shredded - but it was Moorthy who had done most of the shredding.

Over on his side of the defendant's dock, Moorthy Angappan was having none of this. In his version of the affair, he was the hapless victim: completely ignorant of the crime and himself being set up by Vignes, a man whom he had only sought to help out that day, thus putting himself in mortal jeopardy.

According to Moorthy, he had never even approached Vignes' home that evening of 19 September. In fact, he was kilometres away, attending a belated birthday celebration for his nephew in a nearby town most of the evening. The party broke up around 11 p.m., after which Moorthy headed straight home, watched some television and then stumbled off to bed. Exhausted from an unusually long, busy day, he slept all the way through until early the next morning. Not even in his dreams did he wake any time during the night to visit Vignes at the latter's home.

In fact, claimed Moorthy, the first time he had any contact with Vignes in that whole two-day period was around 9 or 10 a.m. Thursday morning. That's when he received a phone call from Vignes asking whether he could travel over to Singapore, pick him up from work, and transport him back to Johor Bahru. At that point, in Moorthy's account, the older man told Vignes it would not be possible right then, as Moorthy might have to make a delivery for a customer.

The one area that the two accused men's accounts agree on is that Moorthy received a second call from Vignes around 12:30pm, asking whether it was possible then for Moorthy to pick him up. Vignes stressed the increasing pain in his leg and his mishap with the borrowed motorcycle earlier that day. Remembering the great kindness Vignes' father had shown Moorthy and his family in similar circumstances three years earlier, Moorthy agreed to try to borrow a motorcycle and make his way down to the fruit shop in Woodlands.

However, when he arrived at the fruit shop, this 'good Samaritan' found himself greeted not by a grateful Vignes Mourthi but by those two CNB agents. In Moorthy's outraged account, he had been framed by the son of a good friend who was using him (Moorthy) to spring himself from the serious charges he faced.

'Serious' is actually a bit of an understatement here. For having that relatively small amount of heroin in his possession, Vignes Mourthi was looking at a mandatory death sentence. And if the state could prove that Moorthy Angappan had, in fact, provided him with the drug, the older man was also set for a date with the executioner.

Sgt. Rajkumar was not taking either man's side on this dispute. In this undercover drug agent's view, both men were guilty, partners - however willing or unwilling - in a scheme to transport dangerous and illegal drugs into Singapore and sell them.

As so often happens in the shadowy world of drug dealers and drug agents, Rajkumar had a string of informers who provided him with tips in exchange for favours and considerations. One of these, the now notorious Tahir, contacted the officer in mid-September and provided him with some juicy information: a Malaysian drug syndicate, composed mainly of ethnic Indians, had a sizeable amount of heroin to move and were looking to sell it in Singapore, where their product drew higher prices than back home.

Rajkumar quickly sprung into action: he told Tahir to try to set up a deal with this syndicate wherein the CNB officer would pose as a very interested potential customer. He even provided the informer with his mobile phone number so that the Malaysian dealers could contact him directly if they so chose.

In Sgt. Rajkumar's account of events, he received notice only at 11 a.m. on Thursday, 20 September that the syndicate had one pound of heroin it was willing to part with for $8,000 Singapore. The CNB officer replied that they could count him in. He was then instructed to proceed with all due haste to the Marsiling MRT (Mass Rapid Transit) station and wait for a call giving him further instructions. After alerting his superior, Assistant Superintendent Krishnan, Rajkumar headed off to the MRT station, where he met up with the other members of this sting operation.

Also there at the station was our old friend, Tahir. Tahir's presence was required as the dealers were only willing to contact the customer on Tahir's phone. The group had assembled at Marsiling by 12:20pm and some ten minutes later, another call came through. This time, Sgt. Rajkumar himself answered Tahir's phone and found himself talking to someone who identified himself as "Vignesh".

This "Vignesh" informed the officer that the meeting place had been switched to the mosque on Admiralty Road, about a five-minute drive away. After establishing how they would recognise each other, Rajkumar hung up, told his team about the change of venue, and they proceeded quickly to An Nur Mosque, hoping they weren't just at the beginning of some wild goose chase.

But the CNB agents were the one group of principals in this tale who were not in for a nasty surprise that day. When they arrived at the mosque, they saw a man lolling about who, Rajkumar suspected, might be this 'Vignesh' he had just spoken to. That's when the officer emerged from the car and presented himself to the young man as the 'Segar' who was there to make the pick-up.

There's a rough concordance between the accounts of the officer and Vignes himself up to this point, but from here they diverge sharply. According to the police sergeant, just after each had established his identity, Vignes brusquely asked where the money was. Rajkumar replied that it was back in the car, with his partner, then asked his own key question: "Where's the stuff?" Vignes replied that he had stashed it somewhere in front of the mosque. He told 'Segar' to go fetch the money, then follow him over towards the mosque.

Having picked up the money from his colleague who was driving the un-marked police car, Sgt. Daniel Chan, Rajkumar rejoined Vignes not far from the mosque. As they headed towards the place of worship, Vignes asked his fellow Tamil how he could trust that Chinese guy in the car. Rajkumar told him not to worry, that this man was Rajkumar's financier. "Without him, I can't deal," the undercover officer maintained.

The two men proceeded just past the gate to the mosque. Rajkumar won-dered for just a moment what was happening now. But Vignes quickly turned around and told the agent the stuff was actually with him; now where was the money. Shown the money and assured that it was indeed $8,000, Vignes pulled a plastic bag from his rider's helmet, where it had been the whole time and handed it to the officer, who in return handed him the bundle of banknotes.

But the officer had one more ploy to put the button on the sting: he asked Vignes if the stuff was good. According to the officer's later testimony, Vignes proudly replied, "It's very good. Watch and see. You are sure to come back to deal with me again." At that point, satisfied that the trap was complete, Sgt. Rajkumar gave the thumbs-up signal. Within moments, the police had their man.

Or did they? After the police had gathered all the evidence and testimony they could collect over a week of gruelling interrogations, it was up to the Singapore judiciary to sort through the strands of conflicting claims and charges and determine the truth of the matter. There was no disputing that

Vignes had turned over a packet containing 27.65 grams of heroin to an undercover agent that day. The key question to be answered was whether he knew that the bag contained heroin.

This was an essential point under Singapore law. If he wasn't aware of the contents, Vignes was looking at an almost certain acquittal after which he would walk away a free man. If he did know, he was facing a rendezvous with the hangman.

Accused and charged with the capital offence, denied bail, Vignes had little that he himself could now do to save himself. He was now absolutely dependent on others, particularly his family and friends. He had no idea just how much help he could expect from his family, with their meagre education, limited financial resources and lack of English. Worse, he had just lost one of his best and most resourceful friends - Moorthy Angappan.

Pursuing The Dream

Over in these parts, they call the Protestant ethic "Asian values". The cultural signposts may be slightly different, but the final destination and the prescribed route for getting there are quite similar: work hard, practice restraint, save and plan, and financial well-being will be yours. It often works, but for all too many over here, it doesn't. After awhile, some of them start to think they've been handed a faulty roadmap to financial well-being and decide to take a shortcut. And one fairly popular - but dangerous - shortcut along the Malayan peninsula is drug-dealing. Which is why many people on the lower rungs of the social ladder elect to take the serious risks that drug-dealing in these parts entails.

27

Most of those arrested for drugs in both Singapore and Malaysia are small dealers or users. And most of these come from the lower economic rungs of society, folks saddled with poor educations and not much money. (However, recently the city-state has seen a surge in the use of 'designer drugs' by young, middle-class Singaporeans and well-heeled expats. In fact, in September 2005, Singapore's health minister announced that three-quarters of recent arrests have been for these new-breed drugs.)

The fact that there have not been many 'big fish' caught in the nets of the narcotics officers merely suggests that those big fish recognise the grave dangers of dealing in Singapore and outsource the transport into the Lion City to couriers and the actual street sales to small-time pushers. The nets Singapore authorities work with rarely reach beyond Singapore's borders.

Chapter 2

MOUNTING A DEFENCE

There is nothing as powerful as the truth and often nothing as strange.

- Daniel Webster

The CNB officers finished with their preliminary investigation a few days later. They were satisfied that they had a strong case. In September 2001, Vignes was charged with dealing heroin, a capital offence in Singapore. As a foreigner with few tight connections in Singapore, he was duly denied bail and remanded into custody in Queenstown Remand Prison in the western half of the island. The fight of his life - indeed the fight for his life - had begun. But Vignes had to sit in a cell, watching it all as a spectator; a very involved spectator, admittedly, but still someone who could only witness the action. It would not be an easy show to watch. (He would remain in the Queenstown facility throughout his trial.)

Vignes arrest not only tossed his life upside-down within a few moments, it also threw the lives of his closest family members into a whirlwind of confusion. Back in Johor, his young wife, Pushpa, suddenly found herself without her husband and main means of support. Vignes' two sisters, who lived with their brother and his wife, were likewise totally confused about where they could turn, what they could do. Meanwhile, up in northern Malaysia, his parents were also about to see their simple lives changed radically.

Vignes and Pushpamalar Thanapalan, known as Pushpa, were married on 19 April 2001, exactly five months before that fateful evening that would spin their lives around completely. Although it had been an arranged pairing, by almost all accounts, the marriage was - up until 20 September 2001 - fairly happy.

Also from the Malaysian state of Perak, Pushpa had moved down to JB to live with her husband and his two sisters. The four young people shared a smallish, one-storey house plunked on a dusty street not far from the centre of Johor Bahru. Jalan Bukit Changar was a dog's-leg of a road with houses on one side, a worried stretch of green on the other. Although she boasted even less formal education than her husband, Pushpamalar was able to find a low-paying factory job in Johor to supplement the household income. (Remember that Vignes tried to send back two-thirds of his monthly salary to his financially strapped parents.) Pushpa also slipped easily into the traditional role of the Indian wife, doing 'women's chores', making breakfast and dinner for her husband almost daily. These chores only increased when Vicky's Uncle Bala moved in with them to help ease their financial strains a bit.

As Pushpa headed home from work early on the evening of 20 September, she was already planning the preparation of the evening meal. But upon returning, she received a distressed phone call from her father-in-law informing her that Vignes would not be home for dinner that evening. He was sitting in detention in a Singapore police station.

The young woman was obviously shocked, and totally at sea. All she could do now was rely on her husband's family and all the friends and support they could muster.

The main arena for Vignes' defence had shifted for a time back to his home country, where almost all his family was. Vignes' parents, siblings and wife had only had limited contact with the legal system hitherto, and nothing whatsoever to do with criminal courts. Now they were thrown right into the middle of the complicated machinery of the criminal justice system - in another country altogether.

One thing his parents did know was how important it was to engage a good lawyer for their son. But how could they find adequate representation for the trial in Singapore while they were living in Sungai Siput, some 500 kilometres north of the Island Republic?

Sungai Siput itself is a sleepy town in the northern Malaysian state of Perak. It lies a bit northeast of the state capital, Ipoh, where Vignes' parents had lived until sometime after their wedding.

In addition to being the capital of Perak, Ipoh is Malaysia's third largest city. Primarily an industrial town, Ipoh's economic life revolves around the tin mines and limestone quarries bunched at the edges of the town. Not far off are sprawls of rubber plantations, which also supply employment for many of the town's residents.

It was on one of these rubber plantations that Vignes' parents met. They were both working on the plantation, as this was a traditional place of employment for those of Indian ancestry in this part of Malaysia. The couple married in 1978. Their first child was a girl, named Kogilam. They eventually raised four children; Vignes was the second child and the only son. As the only son, he held a special place in his parents' hearts. By the time they had started their family, Mourthi and his wife had moved off the plantation and set down roots in Sungai Siput, where they operated a small coffee stall. It was moderately successful, providing enough of an income to raise their small family. However, the family was anything but well-to-do. They often had to struggle just to make ends meet. When the occasion arose, they would supplement their modest income from the coffee stall by renting out a room in the Sungai Siput house. One of their short-term tenants was later to play a major role in the family saga.

Vignes s/o Mourthi (the 's/o' in his name stands for 'son of', similar to the 'bin' in many Muslim names or 'ben' in some Jewish names) grew up in that sleepy hamlet where his parents had moved. He started his schooling at a local school there. He was not a very good student. Neither of his parents had much education, and academics were not stressed in his home.

Vignes father, Mourthi Vasu, was widely known as a kind and generous man - as generous as his limited finances would allow. He had become friendly with Moorthy Angappan years before and the two had kept up the contacts through the Nineties.

Moorthy Angappan had lived and worked in Perak state for a few months in 1997, and during that time, he had rented a room at the Vasu home for three months. This is where he got to know Vignes, then just a teenager. At that point, their relationship was pleasant but tenuous. Moorthy was apparently a good friend of his father's and Vignes found him easy to get along with. For his part, the older man thought Vignes a decent kid. The friendship between Vignes' father and Moorthy Angappan continued after the latter moved back to southern Johor state.

In April 1998, Moorthy Angappan's mother, brother and wife, then three-months-pregnant with their first child, were returning to Johor from a trip north to Perak state when they were involved in a serious car accident, near Seremban in the southern state of Negri Sembilan, roughly midway between Perak and their home in southern Johor. Moorthy himself was, obviously, quite upset about this accident, particularly considering his wife's condition.

When Mourthi Vasu got news of this accident, the older man quickly drove down all the way from Perak to the Seremban hospital where Moorthy's three relatives were being treated, a trip of close to 200 kilometres, to offer solace to Moorthy and volunteer any help whatsoever he could provide.

This apparently close relationship between Mourthi Vasu and Moorthy Angappan formed the basis for the more tenuous connection between the older man's son Vignes and Moorthy.

About a year after the accident, as his only son was preparing to move to JB, Mr. Vasu apparently asked Moorthy to look after him - as he would a younger brother. The long-time resident of Johor readily agreed.

In certain ways, Moorthy Angappan became not a surrogate father to Vignes, but a surrogate brother - an older, much more experienced brother. Vignes even frequently referred to him as his anneh, the Tamil term for older brother. Vignes was still something of an innocent country boy who had not been around the block all that often. Moorthy knew the ways of the more sophisticated, fast-paced border town JB much better. Back in Sungai Siput, Vignes' parents felt relieved that their trusted friend had taken their son under his wing. Moorthy would certainly look after Vignes, they believed.

Although Sungai Siput is not quite 500 kilometres from Johor, Vignes parents suddenly felt themselves extremely removed from their only son. Therefore, one of the first decisions they made was to get themselves geographically closer to the incarcerated Vignes. Low on available options, they decided to relocate to Johor Bahru for the near future. In that bustling border town, they'd at least be just a short bus ride or long walk across the Causeway from Singapore.

But before heading south, they had to do something with their coffee shop in Perak. The notion of turning it over to someone temporarily or simply keeping it closed until they returned was tempting, but not very practical for people in their financial bind. For one thing, they had no idea how long the next stages of the ordeal would last, how long they would have to be away from their hometown. More importantly, they needed money desperately and urgently, to provide the best defence for Vignes they could secure. Ultimately, practicality triumphed over sentiment: the parents were forced to sell the coffee stall which had been their livelihood, a part of their lives actually, for so many years.

Sometime in late December, three months after Vignes' arrest, his parents moved in with his wife and their two daughters. The house they moved into was that squat, rather unprepossessing wooden structure which sat on a dusty road near the centre of Johor Bahru. Despite its dearth of charm, it was still one of the most attractive houses on the street where most of the structures were dilapidated and would soon be torn down in a sweeping program of urban redevelopment. (This house itself was scheduled for the bulldozer in late 2005.)

These are photos of the shanty shack in Johor Bahru in which Vignes Mourthi's family stayed during his trial.

This is clearly not the residence of a fat-cat drug lord.

It was also rather small, comprising four cramped rooms and a kitchen. It was quite a tight fit for the five people then residing there. In fact, when Mourthi moved in, Uncle Bala had to vacate his room and find accommodations with a brother in another part of JB. But the main objective was accomplished: the whole core family was together again, where they could work together to help Vicky. The family may have been of very modest means without much formal education, but they could call on the deep bonds of affection and loyalty of all its members. These, they felt, would certainly play some role in helping to save Vicky.

When they got quasi-settled in with their family in JB, the parents managed to tap some connections and open another small stall located in what they thought would be a prime location: right in front of the entrance to the Malaysian checkpoint for pedestrians or public transport passengers heading over to Singapore. Here Mourthi Vasu and his wife sold kueh, the Malayan peninsula's popular form of cakes and dough pastries.

However, the location did not pan out to be the lucrative spot they hoped it would be. People weren't all that likely to buy greasy or sticky kueh just as they were about to pass through first Malaysian passport control, then Singapore passport control and Singapore customs. Vignes' parents were not able to earn anywhere near as much at this stall as they had hoped they would. Even with the earnings of their daughters and daughter-in-law, it did not look like they'd be able to engage a decent lawyer for their son.

So how was Vignes' family to go about securing adequate legal representation for their only son? Mourthi Vasu would eventually spend about 40,000 Malaysian ringgit (roughly, $20,000 Singaporean) on legal fees for Vignes. But the money they earned from the kueh stall just about covered their ongoing living expenses and left over precious little to engage a strong defence. To get the money he needed for his son's legal costs, Mourthi Vasu had to resort to borrowing money from the region's notorious loan sharks to pay these fees, he later admitted.

This tactic created even as many problems as it had solved. There's a reason why loan sharks are classified as a species of shark: they're not known for their patience or civility when collecting debts. They would often show up at the front door of the house in JB and start pounding on the door, demanding to know when they were going to see their loan (with generous interest, of course) repaid. Moreover, they would often turn up at strange hours.

The banging on the door late at night must have held echoes for Pushpa of that night a family friend came to drop something off, the visit that had set this whole nightmarish ordeal in motion. The next half a year would prove to be a very unpleasant time for her and the other family members there in JB.

The lawyer he settled on for his son's defence was Phillip Lum (a pseudonym). Lum was a good litigator in his own field but had very little experience with capital cases; this case was, in fact, one of his first few cases wherein a client was facing a possible death sentence.

However, earlier in 2001, Lum had been lead counsel in one of the Lion City's more notorious murder trials. In that round, Lum managed to get an indeterminate sentence for his under-aged client who admitted to the actual killing. The client's co-defendant, meanwhile, went to the gallows. In that light, Lum did not seem to be a bad choice. Now it would be his charge to make sure Vignes Mourthi did not receive that ultimate sentence.

Meanwhile, Vignes Mourthi sat in his holding cell in Singapore. Only mildly literate, with faltering English and very little knowledge of the Singapore legal system, Vignes must have felt totally lost. His feelings of alienation and disorientation must have been intensified in knowing that another detainee there in Queenstown was someone he used to turn to for advice and guidance but now could not even bear to look at: his co-defendant Moorthy Angappan.

Tough On Drugs

Both Singapore and Malaysia are known for their tough, even draconian, drug laws. Neither place could be called hospitable to recreational drug users, but they are downright dangerous for those who deal in a wide range of more serious drugs. Possession of relatively small amounts draws the death penalty - a penalty that becomes automatic in Singapore.The authorities of both countries argue, that it is, in fact, these harsh punishments for drug possession that keep their societies fairly clean of drugs, as compared to many other countries (especially in the West, where there is often a grudging tolerance of drugs amongst the authorities and police). But the price borne by those who violate these drug laws - as well as their families - is heavy indeed.

As stated, these figures are just estimates. The reason they remain estimates is that Singapore and many other countries do not supply official figures regarding the death penalty. It is, however, widely accepted that China has the world's highest number of executions annually while Singapore's execution rates would hoist the city-state to the top of the list for per capita executions.

The interesting thing about Singapore's execution practice is that most of those who have been hanged since 1991 were evidently found guilty of drug offences. In fact, in some years, *there were four times, and even seven times, as many executions for drug dealing as for murder and firearms offences put together. (Possession and sales of firearms of all sorts are treated as severely in Singapore as are drug offences.)*

In terms of violent crime, Singapore remains quite safe, so murder and firearms offences, two other areas that carry the mandatory death sentence, are somewhat rare. But it's the drug offences that continue here in large numbers. (The official website of the Singapore CNB reported an astounding total of 3,393 drug arrests in 2002. The vast majority of these were for simple possession and thus not treated as capital offences.) The question of the death penalty as a deterrent for any particular crime is a difficult one to prove one way or the other, but it would seem that the Island Republic's harsh anti-drug laws have not been as effective.

Chapter 3

FIGHTING ON TWO FRONTS

Great contest follows, and much learned dust / Involves the combatants;
each claiming truth, and truth disclaiming both.
- William Cowper (The Task and Other Poems)

The sides were now drawn and the main fight to save Vignes Mourthi began. It was not going to be an easy contest, as the system here in Singapore is weighted against those charged with serious drug offences. (see Box Text)

The trial convened in April 2002. It ended on in August of that year. As is typical of such cases here in Singapore, the two accused men were tried together. More than that, they were seated right next to each other in the defendant's dock. However, it was clear that those warm feelings that had once existed between the two men had disappeared and now been replaced by a deep freeze of mutual contempt. At times, it almost seemed as if the state could save itself the costs of both trial and executions by simply leaving the two alone in a darkened court for ten minutes, allowing them the opportunity to strangle each other to death.

Singapore - A World Leader

Amnesty International estimates that over 400 convicts have been executed in Singapore since 1991. This number, measured against Singapore's population of roughly 4.2 million (including resident foreigners), would give the Island Republic the world's highest execution rate.

Not surprisingly, the two accused were represented by different counsels

- Vignes by Phillip Lum and Moorthy by Lee Teck Leng. No one could ever accuse these two lawyers of working on the same side of this case. Throughout, each of the advocates grabbed any opportunity he could to impugn the testimony of the other accused man, along with any witnesses testifying in his behalf.

In such a twisted situation, the two prosecuting attorneys, lead prosecutor Janet Wang and her assistant DPP Ng, had a somewhat easier job than usual, as both of the defence counsels were involved in handling a large part of their work - tearing at the testimony of and pointing a finger of blame at one or the other of the accused.

The thorny reality of this dual representation in a single trial meant that, in essence, each defendant found himself facing two lead prosecutors, plus two assistant prosecutors, with only one defender (albeit backed by an assistant) in his corner. Over the five months of trial, this constellation of forces was intent on first untangling the various threads of the stories before weaving them back into the picture they wished to present to the court. The untangling and reweaving could sometimes produce a confused picture and presiding judge Tay Yong Kwang had his work cut out for him trying to sort out the facts from the fabrications, insights from innuendos and insinuations.

But he did exercise his authority well in making sure that the story came through as clearly as possible. He would frequently interrupt one of the attorneys to warn him against using tricks or trying to confuse witnesses. Admittedly, Justice Tay warned the two defence attorneys more than he did the Deputy Public Prosecutor and her assistant. But then, as already mentioned, the prosecutors did not have to use so many tricks, as most of the attempts to trip up witnesses had been made by the competing defence counsels.

The first witnesses to appear were the arresting and interrogating officers. With the testimonies of these CNB officers, the trial swept back to that dramatic week in September 2001: the arrest of a nervous and frightened Vignes Mourthi in front of the An Nur Mosque and the second arrest, a short time later, of his anneh, Moorthy Angappan, startled by plainclothes CNB officers as he waited in front of a shop at Woodlands Central. The separate rides for the two accused to the Clementi police station. The transfer to the Cantonment Road police station. The interrogations. The interrogations. The interrogations.

Vignes and the police team involved in the arrest at An Nur mosque all agreed on a few hard facts about the incident. Sometime around 1p.m., Sergeant Rajkumar, undercover, emerged from a silver car, saw a young man limping about and approached him. He asked the young man if he was 'Vignesh', to which the young man replied, "Yes, I am Vignes." He then told the officer that he had the 'thing' from Moorthy. He also asked the undercover officer about the money he was supposed to collect for his friend. At that point, Vignes reached into his motorcycle helmet, pulled out a plastic bag with some granular substance in it, and handed this over to the undercover policeman, after which Rajkumar handed the young Malaysian a thick bundle of banknotes, supposedly $8,000 worth. Vignes took the money. Rajkumar gave the thumbs-up signal. Within moments, a startled Vignes was suddenly seized from behind by two other men and told that he was under arrest.

There was no dispute on any of these facts. The disagreements, which would make up the main body of the prosecution's case and Vignes' defence, was what had happened shortly before these moments, the short time between these facts all parties agreed upon, and what then transpired in the crucial hours and days following the arrest.

Moorthy Angappan's case was even more contentious. All that this defendant would agree to was that he had come down to Singapore to fetch his friend Vignes, still recovering from his recent leg injury, and take him back to Johor Bahru on a motorcycle he himself had borrowed solely for this act of kindness. He also agreed that he was waiting for Vignes near a fruit shop in Woodlands Centre when he was approached by two complete strangers who abruptly began asking him what he was doing there. The next thing he knew, he, too, was taken into custody. Moorthy and his lawyer, Mr. Lee, challenged every other claim made by either the police or Vignes Mourthi.

It was clear from the start that the central drama of this trial would revolve around the two accused, the one-time friends. At the heart of the whole affair was an act of betrayal worthy of classic literature, each side claimed. The version from the Vignes camp charged that Moorthy, who had once served two years in prison, had pushed this young, naive fellow from a provincial nook of northern Malaysia into a plot whose calculating cynicism was almost mind-boggling.

Moorthy Angappan took this fellow who trusted him, even saw him as a guide, an older brother, and used him to serve as his 'mule', transporting the heroin with its automatic death sentence attached into Singapore and from there into the hands of the presumed buyer. When he had assumed that the deal had gone through without a hitch and it was now safe for him to appear, Moorthy rode into Singapore, partly to pick up his injured friend and bring him back home after he had carried out this perilous assignment, but also to retrieve his $8,000 quickly, before anything unpleasant could happen to it. (With all those road accidents, Vignes had certainly been suffering a skein of bad luck lately. Who knew what would befall him next.)

The Moorthy camp countered Vignes' accusations with its own tale of treachery. Vignes had picked up the illicit drugs from somewhere (his lawyer offered one cogent theory in his lengthy submission) and then found himself the victim of a police sting. Shortly before his arrest, when he still believed the entire drug deal was going to run smoothly, Vignes had contacted his trusting 'older brother' and asked him to ride down, pick him up and take him back to JB. Knowing that Vignes was still hurting from his accident, Moorthy decided he had to honour his promise to the young man's father and look after Vignes in this hour of need. In fact, there was a clear echo of the extreme kindness Vignes' father had earlier done to Moorthy's family in this dutiful act of fetching the young man.

However, according to Moorthy's team, by the time the older fellow reached Singapore, Vignes had been arrested. Yes, Vignes was young and naïve, argued Moorthy Angappan's lawyer, but his naïveté was primarily embodied in his belief that making a drug drop in Singapore was a stroll in the park that he could pull off without any problems: meet up with buyer, slip him the drugs, take the money, have a nice day. Unfortunately for Vignes, that's not the way things worked out.

Panicking upon his arrest, the naïve amateur pusher tried to get out of his predicament by grabbing a convenient scapegoat. That scapegoat turned out to be poor Moorthy, who had come down from Johor to do Vignes this special favour. The quintessential Good Samaritan got whacked in carrying out his act of kindness.

The prosecutors' case was a little less dramatic. They, too, saw betrayal in the background, but they chose to split the difference on the duplicity. In their take, the prosecution team saw a conspiracy between the two men. Moorthy was the main dealer, and it was he who had arranged the sale with the shadowy Tahir. To avoid the dangers of arrest, he enlisted the services of his young friend. Then, after the transaction had been neatly carried out, as he erroneously believed, he came down to pick up his mule, collect his $8,000, then head on back to the safety of Johor. Only thing, instead of Vignes, there was a big surprise waiting for him at Woodlands Centre Road. A big, unpleasant surprise, to be a little more precise.

According to the prosecution, the betrayal came only when both men found themselves arrested and, rather than pay blind homage to any code of silence or honour, they decided to save their own necks, literally, by pinning sole blame for the crime on the other one. There may well be honour amongst thieves, the prosecution seemed to be saying, but with drug dealers, it's more often a case of every man for himself.

The first defence witness called to testify was Vignes himself, although his lawyer, Phillip Lum, took the tack of asking that Moorthy be placed in the dock first. This was turned down. Lum did his best to bring the image of Vignes as an exploited innocent into sharp focus. Here was a hard-working young guy, recently married, who was just trying to grab a small part of the Malaysian dream for himself and his family. He was also fond of his older friend and much too trusting. When Moorthy made what seemed like a fairly modest request on that pivotal evening of 19 September, the trusting Vignes immediately said 'yes'.

If his client had made some statements under interrogation that may have indicated deeper involvement on his part, these were just the understandable mistakes of a confused, callow youth. Vignes was obviously very nervous at that point, having been arrested in another country, one known for its tough stance on crimes, particularly drug crimes. He was trying to be as helpful as possible to the police and he was too naïve to see that some of their questions were leading questions or had traps set in them. He may even have signed some damning statements, not fully aware of what exactly he was signing.

When Moorthy's defence lawyer Lee got his chance at Vignes, he went after him with tooth and claw. In fact, early into Lee's cross-examination, there was a lengthy exchange between the judge and Lee in which Justice Tay pointedly reminded the attorney that he was, in fact, a defence counsel and that he should not be doing the public prosecutor's hatchet work for her.

Attorney Lee admitted that while it might have seemed that he was assisting the deputy public prosecutor, he was only trying to defend his client. The best way to do that, Lee explained to the judge, was to undermine the credibility of Vignes so that the court would be more open to accepting Moorthy Angappan's version of what transpired on 19 and 20 September.

To that end, Lee tried repeatedly to trip up Vignes on small matters, hoping every trip-wired step of the way to catch the young defendant in a major mistake, maybe see him sprawl into total confusion, leaving him to slink away from the witness stand with his credibility totally washed away. But despite the battering of hard-edged questions, Vignes managed to survive, if a little more tarnished than when Lee began his questioning.

When it was Moorthy's turn on the witness stand, Vignes' attorney Lum returned the favour, though not with the same zeal and shrewdness Lee had earlier used. Judge Tay did not see fit to warn Lum that he was doing what the deputy public prosecutor was getting paid for. Still, after Lum's barbed cross-examination, Moorthy Angappan also left the witness stand as somewhat damaged legal goods.

Only when Vignes and Moorthy got their turns in the witness stand did the background to the arrests come into full focus. As there was no disputing that heroin was indeed handed over there at the An Nur Mosque in Woodlands, that background - or rather, the two versions thereof - became the battleground for each man's rigorous defence.

That background was stretched back to the time that Vignes had his main motorcycle accident as he was making his way home after work on Saturday the 15th. It was Moorthy who, under cross-examination by the public prosecutor, mentioned that Vignes, after a hard week's work, was apparently drowsy while zipping along on his cycle. He may even have nodded off for a moment before smacking his bike into a curb, which sent him sprawling. As a result, he suffered a rather painful, though not crippling, injury to his left leg.

On that very evening, Moorthy Angappan, accompanied by his wife and two daughters, dropped in on his 'younger brother' to see how he was doing. Vignes told him about the accident, complained of his pain, and then mentioned that his damaged bike had of necessity been left behind in Singapore, not far from the border checkpoint. He wondered how he was going to retrieve it, considering his injury.

Moorthy told him not to worry, that he would come back the next day and help him get the bike back to JB. The older man also enlisted the help of Vignes uncle, Bala, who was then living with Vignes and family there in their small house.

The next day, the 16th, ever mindful of the kindness Vignes' father had paid his family when they suffered a serious road accident, Moorthy returned on a borrowed bike to go retrieve the damaged vehicle. (Moorthy had to borrow this motorcycle from another friend as he had not paid the Singapore road tax on his own bike and therefore would not have been permitted to ride it into the Lion City.)

Moorthy and Uncle Bala rode together to a spot near the Woodlands immigration checkpoint where they found Vignes' bike still sprawled on the side of the road. (Conclusive evidence that Singapore is a fairly crime-free society: in most places, if you left even a damaged motorcycle at the side of the road and came back for it the next day, you'd be lucky to find even a few oil smudges behind, vehicle vultures being wont to suck even those up with straws.)

The bike was obviously in need of minor repairs, which the handyman Moorthy was able to administer. As the gear pedal had been smashed in and the broken light had come out, Moorthy pulled out his tool kit and spare parts to realign the gear and put the light back in. With the bike back in some kind of working condition, Moorthy mounted it and rode it back into Malaysia, dropping it off at Vignes' home. (Uncle Bala followed on the bike Moorthy had borrowed.) While there, he again dropped in on his young friend and inquired as to his well-being.

According to Moorthy Angappan, that day, September 16, was the last time he would see Vignes until he caught a glimpse of him in the Clementi police station on 20 September. But Vignes had a very different version of the time between his accident and their arrests.

Vignes acknowledged the visit of Moorthy and his family on the 15th and the kind assistance his anneh rendered on the 16th, riding down to Singapore to retrieve the damaged bike. He also agreed that he had not had face-to-face contact with Moorthy over the next two-and-half days. But his accounts of the evening of the 19th became the main bone of contention between the two defendants - and the legal authorities of Singapore.

As Vignes testified, early Wednesday evening - the day before he was to return to work - he had gone with his wife to the Hindu temple a short walk from their home. While there, he received a call on his mobile phone from his helpful friend Moorthy. This was around 7:30. Vignes' wife Pushpa answered the phone. Moorthy promptly asked if Vignes was there, as he needed to speak with him. Vignes got on, nodded a bit, then said he would be coming back soon anyway as his wife and he had already finished with their prayers. (When it came her time on the witness stand, Pushpa corroborated this and the following chain of events.)

Shortly thereafter, the couple left the temple and headed back home to meet their guest. The walk from the temple usually took about five minutes, but as Vignes was still limping badly from his leg injury, it took them more than twice as long this time. They arrived back home at about 7:50, walked in to find Moorthy sitting on a couch sharing a drink with Vignes older sister, then exchanged greetings with their guest.

While Pushpa and her sister-in-law were watching TV in a room off the main hall and Uncle Balakrishnan was doing likewise in his own room, Moorthy drew Vignes aside to ask him something. This was the seemingly inconsequential favour he wanted Vignes to carry out when he returned to work the next day. Of course, this particular favour carried great consequences for both men.

After Vignes had agreed to do him this 'little' favour, Moorthy ceremoniously took his leave from all the others in the Indian fashion, going about saying goodbye to everyone personally. He also mentioned that he would be back soon.

By midnight, Moorthy had still not returned. Needing to get up very early the next morning, Vignes decided he could wait no longer and turned in for the night, joining his wife, who was already in bed. After his short, four-day layoff, Vignes knew he would need a large store of energy for that first day back at work following his injury. He drifted off into sleep quickly.

But the couple's sleep was broken about two hours later with a knocking at the front door. A bit frightened by the intrusion of their sleep at this hour, Pushpa, a dreadfully light sleeper, woke up her husband and told him there was somebody at the door; at that point, she had no idea who.

The night visitor was, of course, none other than Moorthy Angappan. Vignes padded past the room off the hall where his two sisters were sleeping and carefully opened the door. A still startled Pushpa had followed her husband out of their bedroom and now stood by the kitchen door staring down the hall to catch a glimpse of their unexpected caller. She felt rather relieved when she saw that it was only Moorthy, the old and trusted friend of the family.

Moorthy apologised for the late hour, explained that he had been held up by the rain earlier that evening, then handed a very drowsy Vignes the packet he had spoken about on his previous visit. He also slipped Vignes a scrap of paper with the name and phone number of the man he was supposed to give the packet to, someone named 'Tahir'. Sleepily, Vignes nodded, said he would take care of everything, took the packet and bade his tardy friend goodnight.

Moving in that state of semi-consciousness that links the worlds of sleep and wake, Vignes casually dropped the packet on the hallway table and headed back to bed. With his still aching leg and the return to work after a four-day layoff just hours away, the young man had more important things to worry about than some small packet that had just been passed to him. Or so he thought. Had he given the packet more attention, he might not have been sitting where he was then, in the accused dock facing a death sentence if convicted on the worst charges.

That, of course, was Vignes' story, both to the investigating officers of the CNB and to the attorneys questioning him at the trial. This story was largely supported by the testimonies of his wife and his older sister Kogilam. (Kogilam had testified right after her accused brother, while Pushpa was on the stand a day after Kogilam finished with her account.) While the testimonies of the two women did differ in certain insignificant details, in all the major points, they corroborated each other on what transpired that evening of 19 September and the two visits by the unexpected guest - as well as the long recitation of events given by Vignes.

(Actually, Kogilam had slept right through Moorthy's second visit. A deep sleeper, she only learned about the nocturnal call the next day.)

Moorthy Angappan did not simply disagree on details with the accounts of Vignes, his wife and sister; he called the whole story of his visits on the 19th a complete fabrication. And his rigorous defence brought in family members of his own to lend weight to his attack on the Vignes version.

As Moorthy told the story, his alleged first visit somewhere between 7:15 and 8:30 was quite simply impossible, as that whole time, he was attending a belated birthday celebration at his sister's home, a 30-40 minute ride from Vignes' residence in JB.

In the saga of September 19 as rendered by Moorthy, he himself had initiated this impromptu party by showing up at his sister's place a little after six with a gift for his young nephew to make up for having missed the actual day three weeks earlier. (He had attended an earlier, official party, but financial problems at the beginning of the month prevented him from buying the young boy a suitable gift then.)

As kids will, the nephew showed his gratitude in part by asking Uncle Moorthy to throw in a little treat as well. Why not, said Uncle Moorthy, who had been both a little short of cash and long on embarrassment when he had missed the nephew's real birthday. And since they were now moving into the realm of a makeup birthday party, why not invite other members of the family over to join in the celebration.

Quick calls were made and within a short time, Moorthy's spur-of-the-moment party had grown to seven adults and a gaggle of children. The party began at around seven and continued on until 11 p.m. The last hour and a half, all the adult males were playing cards while the women sat nearby talking, according to Moorthy. After this, thoroughly bushed, he made his way home with his wife and two daughters, climbed into bed and slept the sleep of the just, right through until mid-morning on the 20th.

Earlier in his sworn statements, Moorthy had claimed that he had not left the party at all until it broke up. The only contact he had had with Vignes throughout the evening were two phone calls, which concerned trying to borrow a motorcycle from a friend which Vignes could ride into work the next day, as his was still not road-worthy.

However, when Moorthy took the stand, his attorney, Lee, served up a few finely-tuned questions that added a little crinkle to this story. The Q&A here clearly established that the ever-helpful Moorthy had slipped out of the party once - to run out and fetch some food at a Chinese take-away stall as well as some drinks. However, Moorthy asserted that this short disappearance had lasted only 30 to 45 minutes, which would have been about the same time required to get him over to Vignes' place, but would leave him no time to wait for the young man, let alone work out the tricky details of that favour and then ride all the way back to rejoin the party.

Attorney Lee soon called three witnesses to bolster Moorthy's version of that fateful evening of the 19th: one of his sisters, her husband and Moorthy's own wife, Satyabama. Satyabama swore that she had spent most of that evening with her husband, while the sister and brother-in-law, the first of the hastily invited adults to arrive at the birthday bash, agreed that Moorthy would have been celebrating with them at the time he was allegedly over at Vignes' house working out the details of the dark delivery.

Moorthy also differed sharply with Vignes on the number of phone calls they had exchanged the morning and early afternoon of September 20, as well as the jumble of subjects they had discussed during those calls. He agreed that he had come down to Singapore to fetch Vignes - but only as a humanitarian act, to help the injured young man whom he had once promised to look after 'like a younger brother'.

Unfortunately, neither of the defendants could produce any exculpatory evidence outside of their own wives or blood relatives. The one witness called by Vignes' attorney Lum who was not related by blood or marriage, Jayacelan Krishnan, offered testimony that could even have backfired.

Jayacelan was the friend who gave Vignes a lift to work on his motorcycle that fateful morning of his arrest. Jayacelan mentioned that when Vignes climbed on the bike he was carrying a small, red plastic bag that happened to brush against his friend's hand. Upon cross-examination by Moorthy Angappan's lawyer, Lee, Jayacelan asserted that this was the only plastic bag that Vicky was toting that morning and "to the best of his knowledge", this bag held a Tupperware container holding Vicky's lunch. However, he was not sure about the contents, as the bag had only brushed against him. He assumed it was his friend's lunch.

Lee later used this information to spin a new theory: that Vignes did not transport any heroin into Singapore that morning, but had picked up the drug later that morning from someone else in the Lion City and this is what was sold to the narcotics officer.

The sharp lines of conflict were now clearly set. This was not a dispute over the interpretation of events and statements or the motivations behind certain activities. Anything that may have transpired on the morning and early afternoon of the 20th was of no consequence if Moorthy had not come over to Vignes' place on the 19th and then returned in the middle of the night in order to drop off that mysterious bag. Which of these two men was lying? Or was it the way the prosecution liked to frame the matter - that both were lying?

The one man who could have shed much light on the whole matter - Tahir, the shadowy informer who had helped set up the bust - never appeared at any time during the trial. This non-appearance of such a key player in the case is every bit as strange as it sounds. Here was a man (and we can still only assume that he does, in fact, exist) who could have implicated or exonerated one or both of the accused. Who had Tahir been dealing with? Had he ever given his phone number to either Vignes or Moorthy? Had he ever worked with either of the two men in a drug deal before this one? What exactly were the arrangements on this one? How did he even know about that huge haul of drugs that the Malaysian syndicate was trying to move? Did the syndicate actually exist?

These were all essential questions that one would think should have been raised during the trial. More, had Tahir taken the witness stand, it would have allowed the two defendants to confront a man who, by his own admission, had been involved in the drug operation at some level. The two lawyers could have questioned him, drawn out more details - including some that might have cleared their clients - and even challenged some of his assertions. Maybe Tahir was himself more involved than it seemed on the surface.

Unfortunately, all of these questions remain unanswered to this very day. In the Singapore criminal justice system, the identity of informants is carefully guarded. Defenders of the system argue that if this were not so, the pool of available informants would quickly dry up. As so much of police work, especially in these days, depends upon prior knowledge of something untoward about to go down, Singapore does not want to scare off any informers. And so Tahir remained, throughout the trial, a name often mentioned but a face never seen.

Possession and Possession

In many regards, the Singapore legal system is a carry-over of the British legal system that was established here over Singapore's century and a quarter as a British colony. Indeed, Singapore defence and prosecution counsels still cite British court and High Court rulings from more recent, post-colonial years in their courtroom arguments.

However, one area where Singapore differs radically from British Common Law is in the presumption of innocence and the burden of proof. To be precise, Singapore largely follows British and most international standards in insisting that a defendant is innocent until proven guilty and that the burden lies with the prosecution to prove that guilt.

But in two categories of criminal acts,

the burden of proof is effectively shifted from the prosecution to the accused. The Misuse of Drugs Act and the Arms Offences Act both stipulate that being found with proscribed drugs or firearms should be taken as proof of either possession or dealing in these products. As major violations against either of these Acts also carries the mandatory death penalty, the situation can be critical.

With regard to the Misuse of Drugs Act, the presumption is that if you are found in possession of above a certain amount of illegal drugs, this is prima facie proof that you were dealing in those drugs - unless and until you can prove otherwise. Further, anyone shown to have been in possession of illegal substances is presumed to know the nature and quan-

tity (roughly) of those drugs. Also, in a case where two or more people are together and at least one of them "with the knowledge and consent of the others" is in possession of a controlled substance, the presumption is that "each and all of them" is in possession of that drug. Moreover, anyone simply found in possession of keys to anything containing illicit drugs or the keys to any premise where such drugs are found is presumed to have been in possession of those drugs.

This matter of possession of keys played a major role in the Shanmugam Murugesu case. Several of the police officers involved in the arrest were asked at the trial if the carrier bags on his motorcycle had been locked and who held the keys to those bags. Each of these officers was asked in turn if Shanmugam had been in possession of the keys and if he had turned the keys over to the officers. By establishing these 'key' facts, the prosecution sought to confirm that the defendant was legally "in possession of the drugs" under the Misuse of Drugs Act.

The section of the law stipulating that anyone shown to have been in possession of illegal substances is presumed to know the nature and quantity of those drugs was a major factor in the conviction of Vignes Mourthi. The young man was clearly in possession of the heroin, though he insisted throughout that he thought the substance was simply incense stones. In both of these cases, along with many others, it falls to the defence to show conclusively that the seized drugs did not belong to the accused.

In another noteworthy case, two heroin addicts were arrested in early 2001 just before the Chinese New Year celebrations. The two men were found to be in possession of more than the prescribed amount for mere users; they were charged as dealers, with the mandatory death sentence tagged on to that charge.

In their defence, the two admitted addicts insisted that the heroin in their possession was indeed intended solely for their personal use. As to why they had such large amounts when arrested, the two drew on the same explanation: during the Chinese New Year's festivities, all the major dealers either return to their homes in Malaysia or Thailand or they spend the whole time with their families here. In other words, the supply of smack dries up to almost nothing during this week-long period. Feeling that they could not make it through the period without an adequate supply of drugs, the two addicts bought enough to tide them over the expected dry spell.

Despite the poignancy and originality of this defence, the court did not buy their story. Both men were found guilty of trafficking in heroin and were executed later that year.

Under Singapore's Misuse of Drugs Act, for a defendant to prove that the drugs in his possession at the time of arrest did not belong to him (i.e., he was not trafficking in those drugs), he has to rebut the presumption that he knowingly possessed and/or was planning to traffic in those drugs. In the latter case, the onus is not on the prosecution to prove that you were planning to traffic those drugs, but on the defence to show that the seized drugs did not belong to the accused. Because of this onerous burden which makes it almost impossible for the defence to prove that the drugs did not belong to the client, a good many people arrested under the Act - God knows how many of them perhaps innocent of the charges - have been convicted. And, of course, many of these convictions have led to hanging.

With so much evidence and testimony, some of it clearly contradictory, some of it inconsequential, it may seem odd that the entire defence of Vignes may have come down to a single word. Was that word uttered during interrogations or not, and why was it not clear that it was or was not used?

The all-important word was sambrani, a Tamil word. As Tamil was the suspect's native tongue, it was the language in which the main interrogations of Vignes Mourthi were conducted. During those very first interrogations carried out at Clementi police station, the main sting officer, Sgt. Rajkumar, and his supervisor, ASP Krishnan, either singly or in a pair, would sit on one side of the table, Vignes on the other. Between them sat that red bag, almost like a silent witness to the whole affair.

Right from the first sessions, the interrogating officers asked Vignes, repeatedly, if he knew what was in the bag. He nodded, trying to be as helpful as he could. It was "sambrani kallu" he told them. Sambrani kallu is the Tamil phrase for incense stones, a Hindu religious incense. It is also the commodity that Moorthy Angappan had once traded in. This was, of course, the spine of Vignes' defence right up through the end of all his court appearances: anneh Moorthy had told him he would be bringing incense stones across the Causeway to turn over to Tahir, not some dangerous drug.

But Sergeant Rajkumar and ASP Krishnan denied ever hearing Vignes say sambrani kallu. According to the two police officers, whenever they asked the detainee about the contents of that red bag, he simply replied "kallu". Literally, the Tamil word 'kallu' means stones. But it also happens to be the street term for heroin amongst Tamil-speaking drug dealers and addicts in Singapore. So if Vignes had only said 'kallu', the chances are good that he was confessing to having knowingly brought in and then sold this drug.

But Vignes asserted that he had always said both words when asked what he thought the bag contained. If that could be proven, the judge would probably have to acquit the young man. But if it could be established that he knew he was carrying drugs, even just as a courier, he would face the mandatory death sentence under Singapore's strict Misuse of Drugs Act.

There was one major problem here for Vignes and his defence. When Officers Krishnan and Rajkumar recorded the conversations they had with the suspect, they only wrote down kallu as his response to their questions. He even signed two such statements. These signed statements amounted to something tantamount to a confession under Singapore law. Based on confession alone, unsupported by any other evidence, an accused can be convicted here. So why would he do such a thing?

The answer is somewhat logical. Here was a young man without much experience or knowledge of the criminal world who was extremely nervous about having been suddenly arrested in Singapore. He was also apparently not much of a close reader. It is quite possible that after making his statements and having them read back to him, Vignes simply failed to notice that the police officers had written 'kallu' instead of 'sambrani kallu'. Such an understandable oversight in such a tense situation could become a fatal mistake if his attorney could not convince the judge that this is precisely what happened.

(One of the lawyers working on his case later pointed out that 'kallu' might not even be a common slang term for heroin amongst Tamil-speakers in Malaysia. Which would be another explanation as to why Vignes did not pay more attention to the difference in what he said and what was recorded.)

This dispute over the terms used could have been easily solved if the two interrogating officers had done their police work a little more thoroughly. As far as any of the records show, they had never instructed Vignes to clarify just what he meant by 'kallu'. If they had only asked, "By that, Vignes, do you mean thoolu (the Tamil word for drugs)?", the question would have been settled one way or the other. Instead, it became a major point of contention between the prosecution and the defence. We can well imagine that in an American TV series like *The Practice* or *Boston Legal*, the police sin of omission in posing this question would become a turning point in the heroes' ultimately getting their client sprung.

Unfortunately, Vignes' lawyer Lum never confronted either one of the interrogating officers with this particular question. So what could have been a turning point remained a non-issue.

Missed opportunities such as this led to Vignes' growing dissatisfaction with his counsel. More to the point, his father seemed to be increasingly disenchanted with his son's legal representation, particularly since the father had scrapped together all the money he could find, even turned to loan sharks, to pay for this defence. Finally, all this dissatisfaction led to another significant development in the trial.

Late in the afternoon on May 9, Vignes Mourthi made a petition to the court to have his lead counsel replaced. The judge, taken aback for a moment, asked the defendant if he had a replacement ready to take over. Vignes replied that he didn't, then asked for three or four days to seek new counsel.

The judge then asked who exactly would be engaged in finding this new lawyer. (As a detainee in Queenstown Remand Prison, Vignes' movements were rather limited.) Supposedly, it would be Vignes' father, Mourthi Vasu, or some associate of his who would undertake the search.

The judge seemed rather skeptical about the whole matter. He warned the defendant, "I know of no lawyer who is willing to take over a capital trial overnight like that." However, a few moments later, the judge agreed to allow Vignes to engage new counsel - but would only give him until 10:30 the next morning to do so! He then adjourned the court until that time, a prudent decision considering that Vignes' lawyer Lum had been engaged in a cross-examination right at the time this request to replace him was made.

(Ironically, just two days before, Lum had mounted an impassioned assault on Sergeant Rajkumar's credibility as a witness, at least with regard to one of the most damning bits of evidence against Vignes. The judge even had to warn him against what he saw as badgering the witness in order to trip him up. Vignes had sought to replace Lum just at the point where his attorney's defence seemed to be taking off.)

When the session opened at 10:30 the next day, Vignes evidenced a change of heart. (No matter how reluctantly he had arrived at that change.) He said he was now ready to continue with Lum. Judge Tay accepted this decision, but he stressed that he took it as a final decision. He pointedly instructed the defendant that he wanted to hear no further protests from either Vignes or his father about his legal representation in the trial.

This matter did surface again, however, late on the afternoon of 16 July, following an almost two-month break in the trial. At this session, Attorney Lum himself asked to be officially discharged from the case because of "allegations of incompetency against me". Lum also mentioned certain "other developments" in his relationship with his client that he could not bring up at that point due to attorney-client confidentiality. However, he did strongly argue that "in the interest of my client" he "should be discharged from acting for him further." A few minutes later, he admitted that the aforementioned allegations against him "had really shaken my confidence".

This time it was Vignes Mourthi himself who was taken aback. He recovered enough, and quickly enough, to make it quite clear to the court that he wanted Lum to continue as his attorney. He apologised for anything he or members of his family may have said against Lum and maintained that he now had confidence in the lawyer to do his best in defending him. More, he strongly maintained that his father supported this decision. At the judge's instigation, he also swore that neither he nor his father nor anyone else would make further allegations of incompetence against Lum or suggest that the lawyer should have been discharged.

And so Lum, despite any shaken confidence, stayed on for the last three-and-a-half weeks of the trial, wrapping up the case as best he could. (These three-and-a-half weeks included a ten-day break.)

There was, however, one major change in the defence team as a result of this controversy. Lum's assisting counsel, Kasturibai Manickam, elected to step down. As Lum wanted another Tamil-speaking lawyer to assist him (to facilitate communication with his client and a number of the key witnesses), she was replaced by Allagarsamy Palaniyappan. (The latter had been assigned to Mr. Lum by the court.)

Nevertheless, the judge's early May refusal to allow more than 18 hours for Vignes to produce new counsel would play a significant role later in the case. But that's for later in this tale.

While most of the arguments on all sides regarding Vignes' knowledge of what he was delivering allowed for a cluster of doubts, one piece of testimony from Sergeant Rajkumar seemed to seal the case against the young man. In a recounting of the actual transfer of drugs and money on September 20, Rajkumar came up with some details that threw cold water on Vignes' claims of ignorance.

This was a sentence-by-sentence account of the transaction wherein the sergeant recalled that after the two introduced themselves, the first thing Vignes did was to ask where the money was. The CNB agent pointed to the car he had just driven up in and said the money was with his partner. He then asked the young man where the "stuff" was.

Vignes told him it was over in front of the mosque, and the two started walking towards the supposed stash point. As they walked, Vignes asked Rajkumar if he could trust the Chinese guy in the car, but the sergeant reassured him, saying that man was his financier and that without him, he just couldn't deal. This seemed to work, as Vignes suddenly stopped in his tracks, reached into his cyclist's helmet and admitted he had had the stuff with him all the time.

Vignes then asked Rajkumar if he had the right amount of money with him. After confirming this, the heroin and the money were exchanged. This is when Rajkumar reportedly asked if the stuff was good. Vignes' smiled and delivered this rather self-incriminating reply: "It's very good. You watch and see. You are sure to come back to deal with me again."

Those three short sentences made it pretty hard to argue that Vignes was just some innocent courier being used by an unscrupulous associate. The prosecution presented this account, taken from the sergeant's field book on the case, as P40, a key part of its evidence cache. But did Vignes ever actually say those three sentences?

They were, indeed, recorded in Rajkumar's field book. However, there was this huge, looming question of when they were actually recorded. The entry itself had no date or time on it, which most official police records do have. It was thus very possible that the reported conversation was written down as much as two months later, shortly before it was officially entered as evidence. The sergeant himself admitted as much.

Defence counsel Lum put great emphasis on this point in his cross-examination of Rajkumar, trying to question the reliability of this piece of evidence as well as the reliability of Rajkumar himself. It was, in fact, during their exchange on this that Lum's defence really caught fire. (see Chapter 13, Aftermaths)

Despite any dip in morale three-and-a-half weeks earlier (when allegations made against him drove him to ask to be replaced), Phillip Lum put together a powerful and persuasive final submission in favour of his client.

This damning evidence, P40, was again cited by the defence counsel in his closing submission. He maintained that the lack of date and time argued against the statement's admissibility in the trial. More tellingly, he pointed out that there was some real doubt that Sergeant Rajkumar had written this entry at all: a comparison of the handwriting of the sergeant's Arrest Report and the P40 record of his conversation with Vignes Mourthi just before his arrest suggested that these were not written by the same person. Lum said that it was more likely that P40 was written by another man, the investigating officer, and put into the field book late to shore up the prosecution's case.

Because of this apparent discrepancy, Lum urged Judge Tay not to proceed any further with the trial but to instead order an investigation into this troubling matter. At the very least, P40 should be disregarded because of the doubts Lum cited. As this remembered conversation also ran counter to all the other recorded statements of Vignes as to his knowledge of the bag's contents, Lum stressed that it should not carry any weight in the judge's deliberations. All the other statements, including those recorded by the police, should override the importance of this questionable bit of evidence.

Attorney Lee's submission in favour of his client, Moorthy Angappan, was no less impassioned and well-argued. Lee also brought out all the reasonable doubts studding the prosecution's case. He also added a theory of his own regarding where Vignes Mourthi may have procured the heroin if not from his client. (Lee, of course, stressed his client's total innocence in the affair.)

Nonetheless, in crafting his verdict, Justice Tay swept aside all the doubts and questions raised by the two defence lawyers. He accepted all the statements of the narcotics officers and most other evidence presented by the prosecution. Accordingly, he pronounced both Vignes Mourthi and Moorthy Angappan guilty of major offences in violation of the Misuse of Drugs Act. The two men were asked to stand shoulder-to-shoulder again as Judge Tay looked down and sentenced both to death.

Trial By(passing) Jury

The reason that the trials of both Vignes Mourthi and Moorthy Angappan were heard by a judge without a jury is simply that there are no jury trials in Singapore.

Although the major elements of the Singapore justice and judiciary infrastructure were inherited from the British system when the tiny republic gained its independence from Britain, trial by jury was one of the features of the colonial system that got scrapped.

The main reason that juries were permanently dismissed from Singapore's courts is the experience of Lee Kuan Yew, the Island Republic's founding father. Before his nation achieved self-government in 1959, long-time Prime Minister Lee had cultivated an impressive reputation as a defence lawyer. In fact, Lee was known as quite an effective courtroom firebrand in his day, often successfully defending those struggling against British rule in the 1950s.

But, says Lee, one key lesson he learned from his days as a hotshot defence lawyer is how easily juries can be manipulated, and with what weak if cleverly weighted arguments they can be swayed. Therefore, when Singapore set up its own judicial system, Lee and fellow members of the founding generation decided they wanted to provide a justice free of emotion and manipulation. The best system of justice for their new republic would be one where all cases were heard and decided by trained judges, not by juries arbitrarily selected for just one case.

In 1966, one year after Singapore had achieved full independence, jury trials were abolished for all judicial proceedings except for capital offences, such as murder cases - in short, those misdeeds that most engage the interests of a community. (The high ratings for locally produced TV *shows recapping Singapore's most notorious murder cases offer strong evidence of this enduring popularity.) A few years later, even these crimes were taken out of the hands of juries and assigned exclusively to professional adjudicators.*

However, through the 1970s, all capital cases were held before a panel of three judges. (Lesser crimes and civil disputes were heard by a single judge.) This was reduced to two judges in the Eighties and then further reduced at the beginning of the Nineties to a single judge, where it stands today. (However, all appeals of verdicts are still held before a panel of three justices.)

As Singapore continues to pursue its opening-up process and its campaign to involve its citizens in the future course of the Republic, a return to the jury system might just get the nod as one important step in this journey.

Chapter 4

APPEALING OPTIONS

Reverence for life is the highest court of appeal

- Albert Schweitzer

But that was just the opening act of the drama. The main action now shifted to Singapore's Court of Appeal, where the two convicted men would get a chance to get their convictions reversed.

Under Singapore law, such an appeal is automatic upon a death sentence. However, in the Singapore system of justice, this appeal takes on major significance, as it is not simply a second chance to get a favourable verdict, it is also theoretically the last chance. Only one appeal is allowed; in capital cases, this is usually the final determination as to whether the accused will, in fact, be executed or not. In murder cases, the appeal hearings can either find the defendants actually innocent of the crime or guilty of a lesser charge, either 'grievous body hurt' or 'culpable manslaughter'

For those charged with drug-trafficking, the appeal can also bring about a reprieve in one of two ways: by finding the defendant innocent of all charges or declaring that the amount of drugs was actually less than the mandatory death-sentence threshold. Neither Vignes nor Moorthy were hoping for the latter ruling; their sole desire was to have the original charge dropped or significantly altered and thus be spared from the gallows.

The appeal against Justice Tay's verdict began on 25 November 2002, or three months after the trial itself had concluded. As is required under Singapore law, the appeal was heard by a three-judge coram: Chief Justice Yong Pung How, Judge of Appeal Chao Hick Tin and Justice Judith Prakash.

For this all-important appeal, Moorthy Angappan was again represented by Lee Teck Leng, assisted by Michael Soo Chia. Vignes Mourthi, however, had new counsel: the celebrated Subhas Anandan, assisted by Anand Nalachandran from his own law firm.

Subhas Anandan is one of the most high-profile criminal defence lawyer in Singapore. In a spate of the criminal cases that make the local TV news, it is common to see Mr Anandan come out of court and address the cameras.

Anandan is, indeed, telegenic in a pleasantly avuncular way. He has an amiable, square face well framed by a scholar's beard with strategic patches of grey in it. Before the cameras, or reporters' notebooks, Subhas is typically low-key, imparting a relaxed, almost nonchalant impression that belies his fine-tuned abilities as a litigator. Upon closer inspection of the man, you can detect that his placid appearance and disinterested scholar's demeanour are a part of his overall strategy: you also get the sense that this is a man whose nimble brain is working in overdrive, playing every angle he can to obtain the best deal for his clients. He was just the sort of lawyer Vignes needed to reverse his conviction.

The attorney did not attempt to dispute any of the surface facts regarding the arrest that day in front of the mosque. He simply stressed the core argument of defence from the trial itself: that Vignes was totally unaware of what he was handing over to the undercover narcotics agent. According to Subhas, the trial judge erred in not giving this naïve young man the benefit of the doubt on his story. After all, the world is full of innocent dupes and people more than willing to take advantage of their innocence.

Subhas also sought to scuttle the prosecution's claim that this argument had been fatally undercut by the testimony of the arresting officer, Sergeant Rajkumar, who had recorded elements of their conversation clearly indicating awareness on Vignes' part as to what he was handing over. (This was that controversial piece of prosecution evidence, P40.) As this crucial information may have been recorded only later, perhaps as much as two or two-and-a-half months later, its reliability was certainly open to question, Attorney Anandan argued.

The implication was clear: the narcotics police, having realised that their case may not have been as rock-solid as they first thought, decided to bolster their case by squeezing in a few more piquant details. Or perhaps it was just that in trying to recall the facts months later, Sergeant Rajkumar might have added some clinching details that never really happened. Negative wishful thinking, if you will. (As we'll see, he did have other concerns at that time.)

Considering that a young man's life hung in the balance, Subhas Anandan argued, the trial judge was wrong in not accepting that these facts certainly contributed to the building of a reasonable doubt as to Vignes' knowledge of what he had carried across the Causeway with him that fateful day.

Moorthy Angappan's lawyer Lee took a similar tack, arguing that the trial judge had been much too willing to accept the prosecution's case, as circumstantial as it was. Lee said that there was certainly reasonable doubt that his client had even gone to Vignes' home on the 19th or the early hours of the 20th, let alone that he had then handed over a bag of heroin to the young man. Although all the witnesses who testified that Moorthy had spent the evening at a post-birthday party for his young nephew were relatives, the doctrine of reasonable doubt necessitated Judge Tay's accepting their testimony.

(Admittedly, four of Vignes' relatives could also testify that Moorthy had dropped by their home on the evening of the 19th and Vignes' wife Pushpa affirmed that he had returned during the night and handed over some packet to her husband.)

The fact that Moorthy had first said the actual birthday was a few days earlier when actually it had been almost three weeks before or that he had at first failed to mention that he had slipped out of the party to buy some extra food were trivial matters that the trial judge should have disregarded rather than take as deciding factors in his decision, Lee argued.

Plus, the fact that Moorthy had come into Singapore four days earlier to retrieve Vignes' damaged motorcycle, repaired it right there at the side of the road and then ridden it back across the border into Johor demonstrated that Moorthy was a man with a big heart ready to literally go the extra mile (or two) to help out his 'little brother'.

In short, the two appeals were essentially compressed versions of the two original defences presented at the trial itself. And they yielded pretty much the same effect. On 22 January 2003, the Court of Appeal unceremoniously rejected both Vignes' and Moorthy's appeals. The three justices in the coram sided with the trial judge, choosing to spurn all pleas to entertain reasonable doubts in favour of supporting their colleague's original decision.

The path to the gallows now appeared cleared of all legal obstacles. The only thing that either man could hope for now was a presidential clemency. This is the one ingredient in the Singapore system which allows clenched-fist justice to relax a little and extend mercy. But what were their chances of getting this mercy bestowed upon them?

The Mandatory Death Sentence

One criticism frequently levelled against Singapore's stringent drug laws by legal professionals is that so many of these offences carry a mandatory death sentence. Those arrested with prescribed amounts of various drugs (and these amounts are often relatively small) are automatically sentenced to death by hanging. There is no possibility of judicial discretion here.

The Misuse of Drugs Act, introduced only in 1977, stipulates a mandatory death penalty for some 20 different drug offences. These crimes include trafficking, importing or exporting various substances on, to or from Singapore soil. The amounts of drugs which automatically call for the death penalty include more than 1,200 grams of opium, 30 grams of cocaine, 20 grams of morphine, 15 grams of heroin, more than 500 grams of cannabis. These limits were all established in the 1977 law. Then, in 1998, Singapore's lawmakers added a mandatory death penalty for the trafficking, importing or exporting of 250 grams or more of methamphetamine.

This lack of flexibility on the question of drug-dealing contrasts with the treatment of other capital offences in the Singapore system. For instance, if you should kill both of your parents, or perhaps a spouse and child, or a business associate and are found guilty, you won't necessarily wind up on the gallows in Singapore. In such cases, the presiding judge and the public prosecutor have the discretion to look at extenuating circumstances and decide that you be tried and sentenced for the lesser offence of manslaughter, which does not carry the death penalty. (Singapore has no categories such as 2nd degree or 3rd degree murder; it's either murder or manslaughter.)

To be fair, it is not that easy for kill-

ers to get a charge reduced in Singa-
pore and most will, in fact, face mur-
der charges and the death penalty.
But of those who are charged with
possessing the proscribed mounts of
illegal drugs, 100% will, if convicted,
be looking at a sure date with the
hangman.

Chapter 5

THE CLAMPS ON CLEMENCY

I have always found that mercy bears richer fruits than strict justice.

- Abraham Lincoln

With the 'guilty' verdict confirmed and a trip to the gallows even more of a likelihood for Vignes Mourthi, his father and other family members stepped up their activities on his behalf. The lives of both Vignes and Moorthy Angappan now lay in the hands of Singapore's popular president, SR Nathan. Under Singapore's constitution, the president of the Republic commands the power to grant clemency, which would at least commute that death sentence to one of life in prison. From there, Vignes and his supporters could try once more to fight for a new trial and, possibly, a complete acquittal on the drug-dealing charges.

Statistically, the chances for the two men did not look promising. A Singapore president had only granted clemency six times in the previous 40 years, the last nod of mercy having come in 1998. The condemned man and his family realised that they had to make an especially strong plea in order to secure one of those rare clemency rulings.

There were really only two ways they could get a positive ruling: they either needed to show why this life was special in a way that the lives of others condemned to die was not. This, of course, is something extremely difficult - if not morally dubious - to prove. The other, only slightly less difficult thing to prove was that the sentence was unjust and thus deserved to be overturned on legal as well as moral grounds. At that point, neither tack looked very promising. Nathan, himself a Tamil Hindu, had not issued a single clemency since assuming the presidency four years earlier. (This assertion is based on the knowledge, information and belief of the author).

In the meantime, Vignes and Moorthy Angappan languished in Changi Prison from late January through August, waiting first for a filing of their clemency pleas, then for a ruling on these pleas to come down. As is true of almost all death row inmates in Singapore, the two Malaysians would be held in a separate underground section of the sprawling prison reserved for condemned prisoners. Their accessible worlds would have been reduced to roughly the three square metres of cell in which they spent much of their day in isolation. The cell would have a toilet, a bucket for washing, a mat but no other bedding for sleep, and no other amenities.

Only in the last week before their execution are condemned prisoners allowed to watch TV or listen to radio. Until that last week, they are permitted one 20-minute visit per week, during which they are separated from their visitors by a thick pane of glass. Their cells themselves are located in the bowels of the prison, bereft of windows, so they hardly get even that restricted bit of sunshine.

This is the severely controlled life that Vignes and his former friend Moorthy would have had for the many months before a decision on clemency came down. All they could do was wait for that literally life-and-death decision. As the months dragged on, it was finally made known that the president's decision on clemency would be made in the near future, possibly the first week in September.

Lawyer Lee Teck Leng again took up Moorthy Angappan's cause and drew up his plea for clemency. Lee had grown even more committed to the cause since the time of the trial as he, too, felt that a possible miscarriage of justice was about to be perpetrated if his client were executed.

Remembering his dissatisfaction with the representation in his son's first trial, Vignes' father, Mourthi, had decided he again needed a new lawyer to take up his son's case. To this end, he had approached J.B. Jeyaretnam, a highly respected former jurist and leading personality amongst many Singaporeans. A co-founder and leader of the Workers' Party here in the city-state, Jeyaretnam was, in 1981, the first opposition candidate to snatch a parliamentary seat away from the ruling People's Action Party after the PAP had gained ascendancy and mass popularity in Singapore in 1966.

However, following a series of political reversals which forced him to petition for bankruptcy, Jeyaretnam was elbowed out of parliament. He even had to pull up stakes and move across the border to Johor Bahru, Malaysia. Here the former contrarian and parliamentarian resides for four days almost every week. The other three days a week, J.B. (as he is affectionately known to his supporters) journeys across the Causeway to his homeland and stays at a hotel in the centre of Singapore.

As he happened to be both a resident of Johor Bahru and a well-respected former Singapore MP with a long history of involvement in human rights cases, Jeyaretnam seemed the logical choice for Mourthi Vasu to turn to in handling his son's appeal for clemency. After taking a quick perusal of the case, the ever-vigilant Jeyaretnam thought he detected a sure violation of rights here and readily agreed to help Mr Vasu prepare the petition to the President.

By early May, the two men had written up what they thought was an effective plea for commuting the death sentence and presented it to the President's office. The appeal was officially submitted in June.

Jeyaretnam's main point of attack was that controversial piece of evidence, P40, which seemed to nail the case against Vignes. (This was the recorded statement wherein Vignes allegedly talked up the high quality of the product he was handing over, even telling the arresting officer that he was sure to come back to him for more.) The former member of Singapore's High Court expressed dismay that this evidence was even admitted in the manner that it was.

As Jeyaretnam stressed, this evidence was not included in the Preliminary Inquiry before the start of the trial, but in fact sprung as a surprise on the defendant and his attorney, Lum. When key evidence such as this suddenly surfaces during the actual trial, a judge should call for the Preliminary Inquiry to be reopened so that defendant and counsel could have notice - adequate notice, to be precise - of all the evidence that is to be presented by the prosecution. That, after all, is the purpose of the Preliminary Inquiry in the Singapore legal system, and Jeyaretnam was baffled Lum had himself not made a stronger protest on the very admissibility of such out-of-the-hat evidence. (Especially as this decisive statement was neither dated nor signed by any of the parties.)

Jeyaretnam also levelled his sights on another key piece of prosecution evidence, P39, wherein Vignes was quoted as saying he believed the bag he was arrested with held "kallu", the Tamil street jargon for heroin. Jeyaretnam not only took issue with how this term was drawn out of Vignes, used in the conversation and recorded (the accused man did sign a statement acknowledging this conversation), but he also pointed out that this key bit of evidence was also excluded from the Preliminary Inquiry and only turned up during the actual trial.

Finally, J.B. reproached Judge Tay for not allowing Vignes and his family more time to engage other counsel when they had made an application to replace Lum partway into the trial. Giving the defendant less than 20 hours to come up with a new defender was "an impossible burden". Because of this decision, Vignes was almost forced to continue with an attorney that (rightly or wrongly) he was unhappy with and this, argued Jeyaretnam, may have robbed Vignes of his full chance at getting a fair trial. For all these reasons, averred the veteran human rights activist, the president should reject the verdict or at least commute the death sentence to a long prison term.

(The last dig was actually rather unfair to Phillip Lum, who had conducted himself admirably as a defender, particularly in the end stretch, despite any remarks that had been made about him by those presumably on his side. His strong final submission was, indeed, impressive and it was in no way Lum's fault that Vignes was found guilty.)

Now all the principals went back to tense waiting. They were aware that appeals for clemency usually take three months before they are decided.

This case was no exception. On 5 September 2003, the ruling finally came down from the President's office: clemency had been denied to both of the men in this case.

There was now apparently no way out for young Vignes Mourthi: his fate seemed irredeemably sealed. Worse, executions in Singapore almost always proceed within a few weeks of denial of clemency.

Some Clarity on Clemency

One other key legacy from British justice, adapted to Singapore's circumstances, is the power of the president of the Republic to grant clemency. This is effectively the last chance a condemned inmate in Singapore has to escape the gallows. However, any decision to grant or not grant clem-

ency is evidently not the president's alone. Decisions regarding clemency are made on the advice of the cabinet, with input from the Attorney General (who is not a member of the cabinet in Singapore's system of government). In a September 2003 interview with the BBC, then Prime Minister Goh Chok Tong described this process at his end: "Each execution comes to the cabinet and we look at it. If we decide a certain person has got to be executed, he's executed..."

While the president's soliciting advice from the various personalities in the cabinet can be applauded as inserting diversity of opinion into the process, many observers see one very big conflict of interest in the arrangement. The Attorney General's office is the group responsible for prosecuting criminals, fighting to see that they get the death penalty for prescribed crimes, and having their appeals denied. That the official who is the head of this office offers input into the president's clemency decisions is...well, somewhat

questionable. Problematic, some would even say.

As mentioned above, presidential grants of clemency are not very numerous in Singapore. Since 1963, even before the city-state became fully independent, there have only been six. The last one, in 1998, was conferred on Mathavakannan Kalimuthu, a 19-year-old convicted of murder. The other five included two female drug traffickers and three murderers.

Several years earlier, a Singaporean president affectionately known as 'the people's president' had issued a clemency ruling, also to a young convicted murderer. When this former president, Wee Kim Wee, died in early May 2005, amongst the many touching tributes published about the man was a feature article in The Straits Times where the mother of the man who was given a renewed lease on life spoke of how President Wee had actually saved her life when he used his clemency privilege to save her son. Such is the power a Singapore president can wield.

Chapter 6

THE LAST CHANCE

Knowledge which is divorced from justice may be called
cunning rather than wisdom.

- Cicero

But there was one more, very faint glimmer of hope: another appeal to get the original verdict overturned and the case brought up for a new trial with a new defence team. The question was, how to build the best team to mount that (perhaps) final defence.

J.B. Jeyaretnam was himself unable to handle the case in court, having been barred from actively practicing law following his official declaration of bankruptcy. (In Singapore, bankrupts are denied certain rights - including the right to practice law - and privileges until they have disposed of all their debts.) But the veteran warrior saw it as a solemn duty to find another attorney who would be able to argue the case as effectively as he himself wished to.

However, the elder jurist knew how difficult finding another competent attorney at this stage would be. For one thing, most legal professionals in Singapore would agree that, following the president's clemency rejection, the legal process had been pretty much exhausted. Few lawyers would want to take up a losing cause, with all the frustrations involved in such a situation - especially as the family's vanished resources meant that the attorney would almost certainly have to handle the case pro bono. Why devote your valuable time, effort and sweat to a losing cause and not make a penny on it?

Moreover, the case was guaranteed to be controversial; indeed, already was controversial. The defendant was an accused heroin dealer already convicted in his earlier trial. Drug dealers do not elicit a surge of sympathy from the general public in Singapore, and those attorneys who defend individuals charged with dealing can suffer professionally. Further, the main points of attack by the defendant's defence team would have to be the incompetence of the original attorney, not exactly an act of professional courtesy at its highest, and the unreliability - indeed, duplicity - of a police officer with many years of service. These factors, coupled with an attack on the way the trial judge conducted the matter, made the final appeal much too hot to handle for most lawyers in the Lion City. The procedural hurdles are almost insurmountable.

Enter R. Martin. An Arts (B.A.) graduate from the National University of Singapore, Martin had gone on to take his law degree from the University of Cardiff in Wales. He had been practicing law back in his native Singapore since 1997. Although he had built up a solid reputation as a dedicated lawyer, Martin did not seem the obvious choice as the lawyer to handle Vignes' case, especially now with the shadow of the hangman's noose looming right before him. In fact, Martin had only been involved with one death penalty case previously: as assisting counsel on a murder indictment. The lead lawyer on that case, was the same Subhas Anandan who handled the appeal on this case. As mentioned above, Andandan is reknowned as one of Singapore's leading criminal lawyers, having handled many of the Lion City's high profile cases in recent years.

In this particular case, from 1998, the defence team of Subhas Anandan and R. Martin challenged the confession statement supposedly made by the defendant and managed to get it tossed out. The murder charge was then downgraded to 'causing grievous hurt', allowing the accused to eventually get off with a sentence of just five years in prison, a major triumph for the defence.

Other than this one shared success five years earlier, attorney Martin was bereft of experience in cases involving life and death. Most of his work consisted of civil litigation and Intellectual Property cases, entertainment contracts and a smattering of criminal litigation

In fact, Martin had not even been paying much attention to the Vignes Mourthi case up to that point. He had heard a few snippets about the original trial from an acquaintance, the female attorney who had been assisting lead counsel on the case before she stepped down shortly before the finale. But it was nothing which had fired his enthusiasm before. Even so, Jeyaretnam felt that Martin was the man to turn to in this case.

The family needed a dynamic lawyer who could take all the drooping arguments they could muster, polish them up and present them in the strongest way, to convince the judges that Vignes Mourthi truly deserved another hearing before the bar of justice. And in this regard, Jeyaretnam decided, Martin was indeed highly qualified.

J.B. Jeyaretnam contacted Martin and arranged a meeting at the latter's office to which he brought along Mourthi Vasu, the inmate's father. This meeting took place on 8 September, three days after the president's denial of clemency to the accused. Timing was essential now.

Martin, a successful lawyer whose success was mainly in civil cases, said he wanted a few days to consider the assignment. He shared a lot of the misgivings that other attorneys would have regarding this case. As he admits, he himself was at first hesitant about taking on the case, and cited five reasons:

1) As the referral came from former opposition MP Jeyaretnam, Martin was concerned that his assuming the mandate might be seen as somehow politically motivated.

2) He realised the case would be emotionally draining, for a wide range of reasons, some of them very personal.

3) He was, of course, aware of his own dearth of experience in the area of capital offences.

4) Following from the two reasons just above, he was concerned that he would be out of his office a good deal, putting much time, effort and energy into this difficult matter. This would mean that he would have to neglect or put off some of his other clients, particularly those paying clients caught up in civil litigation.

5) Although his experience in criminal law was not that extensive, he was all too aware of the procedural limitations he would face as a defender. He foresaw how intractable the system would prove and the impediments he would face in trying to make an effective case for his client. Indeed, under Singapore law, the first appeal on any case is officially also the last appeal.

All these factors told the young lawyer quite clearly that he, too, should just turn down the assignment. However, the factors on the other side were compelling in a very different way. As he read through J.B. Jeyaretnam's opinion in the clemency plea, Martin came to share the older man's view that there had very possibly been a miscarriage of justice in this case. Even so, he realised how difficult it would be to find any lawyer in Singapore willing to step up and try to reverse this miscarriage of justice. It was just too uncomfortable a case for most of the legal fraternity here.

There were also two key personal factors weighing in on the young attorney's decision. For one thing, Martin was a somewhat devout Hindu who had been opposed to the death penalty and animal killing since the time he was in secondary school. On personal moral grounds, he could not square the state's taking a convict's life for whatever reason with his belief in the sacredness of all life.

And one additional factor that plucked at the strings of Martin's heart even more was the significance the month of September held for him. His beloved mother, who had been suffering from a number of serious illnesses for some time, took her own life on September 17, 2000. From that time onward, September had become for R. Martin a time of deep reflection, a questioning of what was most important in life.

Indeed, Martin could not help thinking of his own mother when Mourthi Vasu stood there in front of him. The face of the condemned man's father was etched in pain, pain cultivated over many months time. Although he was only 48, Mr Vasu gave the impression of being somewhat older - clearly the custodian of a large cache of worries. And even though Indian culture generally calls on men to show outward strength at times of great adversity, Vasu could not keep himself from crying at certain points during the discussion. Vasu pleaded with the young attorney to take on his son's defence, even though he realised the paper-thin chances of success. But without a willing attorney, his son had no chance at all.

As he listened to this man make the plea for his condemned son, Martin could not help but think of how his own mother would react if he were in Vignes Mourthi's predicament. As he later recounted, it was almost as if his mother were there speaking to him, pleading with him. It was a powerful association for him.

In short, all the rational reasons lay on the side of turning down the case. But this time, Martin decided to listen to his conscience and not his rational mind. Two days after that meeting in his office, he contacted Jeyaretnam and Mr Vasu to tell them he would, indeed, be taking over the defence of Vignes Mourthi. Further, he would handle the case pro bono, despite the fact that a desperate Mourthi Vasu had offered him $3,000 to come on board as the defence counsel. Knowing the financial hardships the family faced, Martin could not accept the fee, which must have been quite a sum for them, especially considering the large amount (40,000 Malaysian ringgit) they had dished out up to that point.

Martin officially took over the defence of Vignes Mourthi on September 10, less than a week after the president's rejection of clemency. Two days later, a Friday, he was in court for the first of the applications in court to save the young man's life. For all he knew, his client might be facing execution the following Friday, or the Friday after that. To say that R. Martin was under massive pressure is to engage in gross understatement.

The pressure at this first hearing was made even greater by the fact that Martin had not yet received the full records of the trial itself. All he had before him on that morning of September 12 were dribs and drabs of the proceedings, which had come to him piecemeal. In fact, even these scattered bits had been provided to him by Vignes' family themselves, not the court. Nonetheless, for that first court session, this would have to do.

When Attorney Martin accepted the assignment of 10 September 2003, he found himself thrown into the deep end of a morass. Not only did he have to fight his way through all the complexities of the case, with conflicting testimonies and judicial irregularities, but he also needed to straighten out the original case as it was handled by his predecessor, Mr Lum.

Martin duly submitted a 90-page argument in his appeal of Mourthi's conviction. In this document, he especially raised objections to the use of an informer (the notorious 'Tahir') who not only was never called to testify but whose testimony was not even taken for the trial, and the use of P40, that one very damaging bit of undated evidence given by Sgt. Rajkumar for the prosecution. Martin also called into question the adequacy of Vignes' defence team, along with the court's response when Vignes sought to change counsel. In the view of Attorney Martin and other observers of the case, there were enough troubling questions raised about the trial itself for the courts to stay the execution and order a new trial for Vignes. But this was something virtually unheard of in the Republic of Singapore.

Martin was not working entirely as a lone Ranger on this case. For one thing, he had enlisted the services of one of his closest friends from university days, Lincoln Teo, to help out. Lincoln, who had studied Economics at university and was at the time a director of Singapore's Credit Bureau, had mentioned to Martin a few times that he was planning to pursue the study of law. Actually, Martin had been encouraging his close friend to study law from the time the two had finished university.

Martin then started telling Lincoln about this new, interesting case he had taken on. As the two then started discussing the case, and getting deeper into their discussions, Martin saw a spark in Lincoln's eye. He presented Teo the challenge of being 'near the action' on some exciting judicial proceedings. Martin insisted that being 'down in the trenches', seeing how such a case would be put together and argued was even more valuable than any traditional law course could be. Teo gladly accepted the challenge.

A few days before the first hearing, Martin travelled up to J.B. Jeyaretnam's home in Johor to meet with the senior lawyer and he invited Lincoln Teo to join him. Lincoln drove up with his wife, and Martin rode with them. They arrived at Jeyaretnam's place around 9 p.m. and, over dinner, the veteran fighter gave Martin some valuable advice on how to present the application for a stay of execution as well as some good ways to pursue the case from there.

The three men discussed the matter until after midnight. Jeyaretnam had advised Martin to take the case directly to the Court of Appeal, but Martin changed this strategy, feeling that it would be foolhardy to go into the court that had already rejected this defendant's appeal and hope for a reversal. (Especially as he still had not received the records of these proceedings.) Martin felt that by fighting motions directly before the High Court he could attract the attention of the Appeals Court as well as highlight the human rights issue.

Lincoln Teo continued with the case all the way, meeting up with Martin almost every other day to see how he could help out with the small things necessary to argue an effective case. (This, despite his time- and energy-consuming day job at the Credit Bureau.) The old friend would run over to Martin's office during lunch breaks or at the end of the working day to see what he could do.

Teo recalls that the attraction of this case for him involved a mix of adventure and righteousness in the sense that the two old friends felt this case deserved to be pursued to the fullest extent of the law so as to ensure that the defendant would not hang until every possible point had been heard and weighed in a court of law.

The 12 September hearing was set for 10:30. It was only a few minutes before the start of the proceedings that R. Martin actually met his condemned client for the first time. (Martin never actually saw Vignes at Changi Prison. All their meetings took place at the courtroom.) As Vignes settled into his seat in the defendant's dock, the young man looked surprisingly cool and calm. He had a dark, broad face framed by a healthy shock of hair and tightly trimmed beard.

Martin walked over to the witness dock and leaned over the side to shake hands with his client. Vignes smiled warmly at his new lawyer as they introduced themselves to each other. The defendant extended both of his handcuffed hands, then stretched the right hand a little further to shake hands with his new counsel. Martin smiled back at him, then shook his constrained hand. There was a kind of instant rapport between the two.

Vignes' father had already told Vicky a bit about this new lawyer he had managed to engage. The bond between them flowed from several sources: both spoke Tamil and they had both come from humble backgrounds. (Martin had, of course, managed to rise from his own humble background.) This kind of affinity was essential for success at this late date. As Martin emphasises, "You need to feel the pulse of your client." Martin quickly sensed that he knew the pulse of this client, which would make his difficult task just a little easier.

There was also a kind of buoyancy in Vignes' smile, even a different atmosphere in the high-ceiling room. This was, indeed, a new chapter. This would be his first Singapore court appearance where Vignes was not sitting next to co-defendant and ex-friend Moorthy Angappan. For the first time, Vignes could anticipate having his account told on his own terms. Today, he didn't have to worry about a second defence lawyer sniping at his position from the rear. For this reason alone, Vignes sat more comfortably in his chair at the High Court as the session was about to begin.

Nonetheless, Vignes leaned over and admitted to his new attorney that he wasn't very hopeful about getting a favourable ruling from the court. Still, he was overwhelmingly grateful for the efforts that his family and the lawyer were making on his behalf. This was especially so as Vignes still saw himself as a hapless victim of injustice.

Also at this important hearing were Vignes' immediate family members - his mother, father and all three of his sisters. As the hearing got underway, all five of them looked tired, drained, showing clear signs of the stress they had been under, particularly over the past week. Yet, they also had strong pleading looks on their faces. Their looks seemed to ask the court to save their son's, their brother's, life.

The presiding judge at this hearing was Justice Woo Bih Li. When Martin learned that Woo would be ruling on his application, he felt a heavy thud in his stomach. Woo was known as a tough jurist. Having him on the bench would not make Martin's difficult task any easier.

With all the pressure on his shoulders, R. Martin had come into the courtroom already on edge. Engaged in a fight for his client's life, he knew all too well that the only way to win such a fight was to come out with fists flying (metaphorically, of course). The niceties one often found in civil litigations and IP cases would have to be dispensed with in this situation. This was a different game altogether. He was also in the thick of preparing a five-day High Court trial between the 22nd and 26th of September 2003.

Martin asked the court orderly if the hearing on his unusual application could begin straight away. He wanted to get the rhythm of the hearing working for him, especially considering his adversary that day. Handling the case for the government was Deputy Public Prosecutor Bala Reddy, assisted by Francis Ng.

Mr Bala Reddy was both Senior State Counsel and Deputy Public Prosecutor in the Attorney General's Chambers. In effect, Reddy was one of the top guns on the Attorney General's team. He stands as a formidable opponent for any defence lawyer, especially one with scant experience in capital cases. An alumnus of both Cambridge and Harvard Universities, where he obtained his LLM and M.Phil degrees, Mr. Reddy is known for having handled a number of contentious cases, including those involving free speech issues and various drug offences. He also teaches Criminal Procedure at the Postgraduate Practice Law Course. For his many services, Reddy was conferred the prestigious Silver Public Administration Medal in 2002. (In July 2005, he was promoted to the post of a District Judge)

In the courtroom, DPP Reddy came across as a generally cool, bottom-line, straight-to-the-point litigator. He rarely wastes any smiles on his legal opponents. The tension between Reddy and the defence lawyer was apparent right from the start.

Francis Ng is another of the top guns in the department. He is known for his sharpness, his attention to small details and his ability to nail a defendant. By assigning these two to the case, it was very clear that the Attorney General's office, having advised the president on granting clemency to Vignes Mourthi, did not care to see the entire case reversed or even brought up again in a new trial.

R. Martin tried to break the professional ice between the two as the hearing got under way by asking humorously, "Bala Reddy, are you ready?" The Deputy Public Prosecutor did not even respond to this, but got right down to the business at hand.

DPP Reddy rose confidently and argued that the application for retrial was itself misconceived as both the criminal case and the official appeal had been held and dealt with according to the law. For that reason alone, Reddy went on, the High Court actually had no power to order a retrial or a stay of execution.

Defence Attorney Martin, of course, took objection to this reading of the law. He and Reddy were soon trading swipes at each other's positions. After a few sharp exchanges between the two attorneys, an impatient Judge Woo ordered both of them to "stop all this nonsense". This was a signal to all parties present: abundant patience was not on the judge's agenda that day.

Martin began his defence by asking for a six-week adjournment, pointing out that he had been engaged by Vignes' family just two days before, had met his client for the first time just prior to this hearing, and needed the six-weeks grace period to consult a Queen's Counsel.

Justice Woo showed little sympathy for the situation of either Martin or the prisoner facing imminent execution. He acerbically replied, "Don't you think you should have done all that before you filed the application?"

To this, Martin argued that he had had to act quickly, as the president had already turned down Vignes' appeal for clemency. As he was preparing the case, he actually feared that his client could have been taken to the gallows as early as that very Friday morning. He also conceded that he wasn't actually sure that the High Court was, in fact, the right venue to make his case as he had only been instructed 2 days prior.

But Judge Woo brusquely countered that he saw no sense in granting an adjournment of the case, as the application itself was faulty. This case didn't belong in the High Court at all, declared Woo, as there had already been a ruling from the Court of Appeal, which is the body responsible for such matters. It was now quite evident that the animosity between the defence and prosecuting attorneys was not the only animosity in the court that day.

Nevertheless, Attorney Martin vigorously stated his stand on the application. At this stage, Judge Woo issued a warning that counsel should "watch his tone".

As Martin then proceeded to make his case, Judge Woo tried to cut him off, always coming back to his default position that his court was not the proper venue for such arguments. Further, as the judge saw it, the case had already run its course. But R. Martin had not come to court that day to just throw in the towel and tell the family to forget the whole matter. He continued to press on with his arguments. With pursed lips, the judge sat back and listened until the next opportunity to interrupt.

The hearing lurched on for some two hours. Several times during the proceedings, Martin sat down while the judge was taking notes of what had been said. As it sometimes took the judge several minutes to write down his notes, Attorney Martin felt it pointless to remain standing throughout as he was also taking down notes and suffered from slipped disc. At one point, Woo noticed that Martin was seated and gruffly asked the attorney to "please rise". Martin then asked if the judge himself could speak more politely.

This acrimonious atmosphere continued throughout the hearing, with all three legal parties sniping at each other. In a moment of exasperation, Judge Woo told Martin, "In fairness to you, I am alerting you that I find your conduct improper and that I have to make a complaint to the Law Society."

To this, R. Martin shot back with a retort that sent out ripples throughout the local scene for the next month or so: "That's fine. I have no fears. That is why I am here."

This raised many an eyebrow around the courtroom. And there were more than the usual number of eyebrows present for a Friday morning session. On that morning of 12 September, there were perhaps another twenty lawyers making pleas and applications of various sorts. When they heard about the nature of this particular case and felt the tension in the air between the principals, many of them decided to stay around and see how the play of forces unfolded. It was almost like passers-by staring at an impending accident: they could sense that something unpleasant was about to happen and they didn't want to miss it.

The show proved well worth the stay. When warned by the judge that he would be facing a complaint to the Law Society, Attorney Martin issued a warning of his own: he said he would be filing a complaint to the Law Ministry about the judge's behaviour as he was certainly "entitled to speak" under Singapore's constitution.

All this time, the defendant Vignes was transfixed, even entertained. Though his English was not all that strong, he could feel the energy and zeal being poured into his defence by this new attorney. This was quite different from the low-voltage approach taken in the original trial. Vignes and the other members of his family - whose English was even weaker than his - started to believe that maybe their cause might prevail in this round, though they were advised not to have any hopes, but rather to never say die.

But any swell of hope was soon quashed. At the end of the presentations, Judge Woo coolly dismissed the application for an adjournment, saying he could not see how a delay would serve any purpose. The judge then shrugged, rose from the bench and disappeared into his chambers.

A bit calmed down now, and perhaps reconciled to the inexorable process of the sentence, R. Martin told the judge, as well as some reporters encircling him at the end of the hearing, that he would not, in fact, be making any complaint to the Law Ministry. He then added that the reason he would not be filing a complaint was that he was "leaving the country; I'm planning to migrate to Australia."

Attorney Martin, who is still today a Singapore resident as well as citizen, later explained his 'emigrating to Australia' comment this way: "I was frustrated with the criminal justice here and was actually making plans to emigrate. I wanted to show the court that I had other options. I felt like, if I can't argue my case here, what is my role in the court? Why am I here?"

As Vignes Mourthi was escorted out of the courtroom, a sharp air of disappointment clouded his features. Though he had not been very hopeful at the beginning of the session, he was even less so now. And this was a large drop from that surge of optimism he had been riding on a short time before. He fully knew that, with the failure of this application, he could be hanged one week from that day. Attorney Martin was also aware of this dire possibility and conveyed that fact to Vignes' father. Nonetheless, the lawyer, the family and Vignes himself decided to press on with the fight, to grasp at any straw they could to first postpone and then escape the hanging altogether. However, the Singapore legal system did not provide them with many remaining straws.

Martin did clutch at one possible straw: he promptly took out a second Criminal Motion asking for a postponement and a retrial. It had been a long, anxious weekend, and all those involved on the defence side breathed a heavy sigh of relief when there was no execution date released for the week of 15 September. This meant that Vignes and his team still had at least two weeks left to save his life. With this in mind, Martin quickly prepared another application for a hearing, which he submitted on the 17th of September. A hearing was then scheduled for that Friday, the 19th, exactly one week after the acrimonious session in Judge Woo's court. In the meantime, R. Martin had been able to acquire the full court records of the original trial. These were provided by the Supreme Court Registry itself. But it was hardly an act of overwhelming generosity: the court issued the attorney a CD-ROM of the trial, then charged him $800 (Singapore dollars) for the disc!

Back at the prison, a new, hopeful leitmotif had brightened the outlook a bit - even though Attorney Martin had told them quite plainly after that first hearing that their chances were almost nil. Vasu had gone to visit his son at Changi on Monday, the 15th of September. At this meeting, Vignes had told him "Appa (Papa), I am going to come home." And this time, he seemed to believe it. Having seen a lawyer in his corner who was fighting so hard, obviously so deeply involved in his case, Vignes began to again feel that his cause was not hopeless. (Despite the dire warnings from this lawyer himself.) This buoyed the father, who the next day told the Malaysian newspaper Malay Mail, "Those words meant so much to me, because my prayers have been answered." But was he speaking too soon?

Attorney Martin was also somewhat buoyed when he arrived at the courthouse early on the morning of 19 September and discovered whose courtroom the hearing was to take place in. Reading the hearing schedule, Martin perked up; a more sympathetic arbitrator, Justice Lai Kew Chai, would be presiding judge at this hearing. On the other hand, Martin would be facing the same adversaries across the bar table - the brilliant DPP Bala Reddy, backed up by the formidable Francis Ng. But at least he wouldn't have to take on both a tough prosecutor and an unsympathetic judge.

The courtroom was jammed with journalists and fellow lawyers. There wasn't a free seat to be found. Even two of Martin's family members - his eldest brother and youngest sister - were unable to find seats for this tension-packed hearing. Finally, after much searching, the sister did manage to squeeze in along one bench. His brother had to leave at first, since the court does not allow spectators to stand. He could only get back in to watch his younger brother in action when some other attendees had left and he was able to take one of their seats.

Most of the spectators were lawyers and members of the bar, about 40 or 50 in all. The unusually large contingent of journalists came mainly from Malaysian publications, drawn by the drama of a compatriot facing the gallows in Singapore - perhaps unjustly. (Had it been a Westerner or a citizen of a western country fighting to escape execution, the press contingent would have probably been even larger, with many representatives of the international media flocking in to observe Singaporean justice at work.)

But the most important thing for Attorney Martin and his client was that they would get a fair hearing in which they could finally raise the points of law involved. Also, if the application was rejected, Martin hoped that the reasons would be stated clearly and cogently and the principles applied accordingly. (This, he conceded, was the court's prerogative. He just wanted fairness and transparency.)

Vignes and his family again attended this hearing. Vignes had been led in by three police officers, who again escorted him to the defendant's dock. Though handcuffed, he was not shackled as he entered the dock.

When Vignes saw his new lawyer this second time, he looked extremely happy, just knowing his case was getting this whiff of fresh air. He also enjoyed a literal whiff of fresh air, as any trip out of the confines of the prison walls into the centre of town and an excitement-charged room was something of a treat for this young man who had spent the last two years in either remand or prison.

Indeed, the whole proceeding provided a spark of excitement for Vignes, just being there in the court, surrounded by a large number of people who were not dressed in either inmates' togs or prison guards' uniforms. He was actually surprised to see so many people in attendance, the majority of them strangers, and assumed that most of them were on his side.

Despite the odds that he faced, and remained well aware of, Vignes Mourthi was beginning to see some further rays of hope that the sentence meted out to him might be reversed. (As the British like to put it, by this point, he was more 'exhil' than exhilarated) Interestingly, Vignes never once asked Martin point blank what his chances were. Maybe he felt that asking would in some way curse whatever chance he might have.

In contrast to the first justice, Judge Lai did not interrupt Martin a single time as the counsel carefully laid out his case. He did, however, ask a few incisive questions to elucidate key points. Justice Lai may not have been sympathetic to the cause the attorney was fighting for, but he was clearly ready to lend a thoroughly fair hearing to that position.

Martin held forth for close to two hours at the start of the morning session, then gave way to DPP Reddy, who argued for 30 minutes. After the lunch break, Martin offered a 30-minute rebuttal to Reddy's case, then rested.

In his presentation, Martin again brought up the issues of a possible miscarriage of justice. Among the new issues raised were that the elected president of Singapore was made accountable to parliament with wider powers, including the power of clemency. Martin introduced the theme of Article 22P of the city-state's constitution (added in 1991, when the constitution itself was amended), arguing that this passage must have some bearing on giving wider powers to the president. Further, these powers should be used in cases such as the one now before the court.

Delivering his submission, DPP Reddy again maintained that the High Court had no authority to entertain the motion presented by the defence. He cited three previous cases where Singapore courts had ruled that no further action could be taken after the Court of Appeal had made its decision. Reddy stood on what he felt was the unshakeable ground of legal procedures and their fixed nature.

Martin then reached into the bag of human justice principles and gamely asked Reddy if this meant that an innocent person could be hanged because of procedural regulations. The Deputy Public Prosecutor, shrewd litigator that he is, must have realised he was being asked to take a short stroll into an ethical minefield and deftly sidestepped Martin's question. And then it was lunchtime. It was also time for the defence to plot its counter-attack on the state's position.

But at least the defence counsel didn't have to worry this time about covering his flank as he attacked. Martin was duly impressed with Lai's fairness and openness in this hearing, especially after the atmosphere and treatment that had prevailed during the earlier hearing.

He recalled his now famous comment that since he could not argue his case fairly, he was planning to emigrate to Australia and said that he was now convinced he should stay in his homeland of Singapore. "I'm thrilled to find judges here like you," Martin told Justice Lai, "which makes me reconsider my decision to emigrate to Australia." At this, the courtroom broke into laughter and applause. Lai himself was "pleased as punch" to hear this, though his embarrassment at the unexpected compliment caused him to turn a fine shade of crimson.

The attorney added that he saw Judge Lai and himself as two wheels of a carriage rolling to prevent a miscarriage of justice. This brought laughs from almost all in attendance, including Justice Lai Kew Chew, who contributed to the laughter when, looking straight at the defence attorney, he chimed in, "I hope that one wheel does not think it is bigger than the other."

As they were returning from the lunch break, Martin and Justice Lai happened to run into each other on the street, heading in opposite directions.

As they passed, in a sign of mutual admiration, they both took exaggerated bows of reverence to each other.

This hearing certainly lacked the acrimony of the earlier session, but the results were no less bitter for Vignes, family and friends. Justice Lai's main concerns were that, according to Singapore law, after the Court of Appeal has exercised its jurisdiction, you cannot bring a new point to the court or ask the court to review the facts of the case.

Although Martin had argued cogently that this court, too, held the 'inherent jurisdiction' and revisionary powers to entertain a criminal motion even at this late date, Justice Lai believed that his court had no authority to rule on this matter. Despite his sympathetic demeanour, he finally concurred with DPP Reddy and, agreeing that he had neither the jurisdiction nor the power, he dismissed the motion. Another major defeat had been placed on the shoulders of Vignes Mourthi, his family and his defence team.

Martin had earlier emphasized to Judge Lai the circumstances of his coming on board as Vignes' lawyer. He further stressed that even though he now had the full records of the trial (after paying that $800 out of his own pocket for a CD-Rom, which he did not shrink from mentioning), he still needed some time to make the most effective case for his client. But even that, the simple plea for more time, was not entertained. As fair and open - even pleasant - as he had been, this judge, too, failed to express any sympathy at all for the argument offered by the defence.

As the hearing reached its conclusion, with the judge's dismissal, Martin turned to look at his adversary, Bala Reddy, but Reddy did not so much as throw a glance in Martin's direction. As the defending attorney recalled later, "I don't think he wanted to look at me at that point." Having successfully fulfilled his duty, Reddy simply turned and walked out of the courtroom without even nodding at his legal opponent.

Only at that moment, when this appeal, too, was dismissed, did this essential fact hit Martin fully: his client would probably be hanged in a week's time.

Meanwhile, the court interpreter leaned over and started explaining to the defendant what the judge's ruling meant. Vignes listened attentively, and after a few moments, a look of shock, mixed with confusion, fell across his face. Tension racked his body. He had felt that after being given a fair hearing by a fair judge, he would certainly be granted a stay of execution. That's all he expected at this point, a stay. But even that had been denied him.

The condemned man turned around and stared at his father, then standing a mere ten metres away. The older man was on the verge of tears, which increased his son's own despair and anxiety. A forlorn look crossed Vignes' features.

Within moments, R. Martin strode up to Vignes and put a hand on his arm; the latter started to recover almost immediately. The tension ebbed out of his face and the rest of his body. He felt in this gesture, along with the attorney's words, that there was some hope. In fact, he looked around again to his father and told him once more that he would be coming back home. However, immediately after this promise, the handcuffed convict was taken by the three policemen attending him and led off to the van that would return him to Changi Prison.

As Vignes disappeared down the special staircase reserved for those charged with serious offences, his mother and his three sisters looked extremely dejected. None of the family members could speak anything more than minimal English, so most of the foregoing proceedings had been lost on them. They were hanging on the judge's every word without being able to fully grasp what he was saying, but were well aware that the fate of their loved one was being spun out in those words.

Martin went up to the family and explained to them the situation in detail, including any remaining options they might still have. At the same time, a number of other lawyers in attendance approached Martin, shook his hand and congratulated him on his presentation.

Martin turned back to the Mourthi clan. All five members of the family were now in tears. As the lawyer was himself on his way to the nearest Hindu temple, he invited them to join him there for prayer and supplication. They agreed readily. The temple they adjourned to was the famous Sri Mariamman in Singapore's Chinatown, which happens to be the oldest Hindu temple in the Lion City. Sri Mariamman herself is, coincidentally, the goddess of compassion, justice and democracy, and many Hindu devotees make their way to this temple expressly to pray for justice or the rectification of some injustice.

Following their prayers at the temple, as Martin recalls, "we all went home." But it would be a painfully long weekend for Vignes, his family and R. Martin. Would the dreaded execution order come on Monday? Would they have another week, another two weeks, another...

On Monday, 22 September, these gnawing questions were answered: Mourthi Vasu received a short notice from the superintendent of Changi Prison informing him, in clipped offialese, that his son would be executed that coming Friday.

Vignes and his legal team were fast running out of cards to play. (And the Singapore legal system has far fewer cards in its deck than many other jurisdictions.) The letter also mentioned that Mourthi and other family members could visit the condemned man at the prison daily from the following day,

Tuesday, until Thursday, one day before the scheduled execution. (The limit of one 20-minute visit per week was lifted for these supposedly last few days.) Further, the family could pick up the body a few hours after the hanging and arrange for the funeral. If they didn't or couldn't, the state would cremate the body. Unless R. Martin was able to pull off a judicial miracle - or some other kind of miracle - Vignes Mourthi would be dead by the end of the week.

But Martin refused to accept this likelihood; He now swung into overdrive. Fortunately, right around this time some unexpected but much needed help came R. Martin's way.

MG Guru, an ex-lawyer, happened to read the article in The Straits Times on the first hearing and Martin's confrontation there with Justice Woo. Guru later recalled how impressed he was that this young lawyer had the courage to stand up to the High Court in that way, which - he added - was something extremely rare in Singapore.

Early that morning, he told his wife, "There's one young lawyer, a very brave lawyer, oh, what a great thing - at least justice is not dead here. It's still around." But he left the matter there. However, a week later, he saw another article, this time reporting on the second hearing and Martin's more amicable dealings with Justice Lai Kew Chai.

At this point, seeing that the brave young lawyer was still up on his feet fighting on his client's behalf, Guru himself got inspired and decided to join in. Although he had not practiced law in ten years, Guru wanted to jump into this high-profile case and contribute in any way he could.

He contacted a lawyer friend of his and asked how he could get into contact with Martin. This lawyer friend gave Guru the telephone number for Martin's clerk. He then called up the young lawyer on Saturday, 20 September and left a message. Martin subsequently returned the call. Guru told

Martin about his legal background and offered any assistance he could provide. They agreed to meet up later that same evening and discuss the next steps in the campaign to save Vignes Mourthi's life.

Martin and Guru met for dinner that evening at a restaurant on Serangoon Road in the Little India section. At this meeting, Martin brought the older man up to speed on the case and handed him some of his notes. They agreed that the best way for Guru to help at this point would be to do some of the crucial research work, freeing Martin of this time-consuming burden. Guru offered to do the work pro bono, as he knew the young lawyer was himself handling the case on this basis. But Martin was so grateful to get this vital assistance at this critical point that he graciously told Guru he could submit a bill for any services rendered.

Guru could not have appeared at a better time, as Martin was truly feeling swamped with the work he was putting into the case. Not only was he doing research almost around the clock, he was also still fasting in preparation for the Hindu firewalking ceremony. The fasting and the heavy workload had combined to bring him to a near state of exhaustion. If we can think of our store of energy as a bank account, Martin at that point was clearly overdrawn but just hoping that he could continue drawing on his energy credit line and repay

Motion Slickness

The reason that R. Martin filed a criminal motion rather than an appeal in this case is that the appeal had already been heard, back in January of the same year. In Singapore, once an appeal has been heard and rejected, there are no further appeals possible.

A criminal motion is a manoeuvre outside the legal mainstream. It seeks to address a possible irregularity or anomaly in the original trial - or in the system itself.

these borrowings later.

Early Monday morning, Guru made his way to the research department of the Singapore National Library to carry out his research. He worked for over twelve hours digging up the research, only ending around 9:30 p.m. as the library was about to close for the day. He was able to find a number of relevant cases and come up with a batch of helpful pointers. The following day, he met up with Martin and gave him all the pertinent research material he might need to further bolster his case.

Martin intended to collate all this information, but then discovered that all the other pressures around this case prevented him from doing so. (Keep in mind that Martin had other cases he needed to attend to during this period. He couldn't simply toss out his paying clients in favour of this pro bono case.) He then asked Guru if he could provide some further assistance in writing up this material. The older man, now quite energised by the case and all its implications, readily agreed.

The next day, Wednesday the 24th, Guru went to Martin's office and, assisted by the latter's secretary, wrote up the relevant materials. He again put in twelve hours of dedicated work on this, helping prepare the substantial legal research for the submissions Martin would make the next day. He left late Wednesday evening knowing that he had done everything he could to help clear what he now believed was an innocent man. Everything now rested in Martin's hands - and those of the three judges he would face the following day.

Chapter 7

THE FINAL HEARING

Is he "still maintaining that an innocent man can be hanged because of
procedure?"

"Yes; the answer is yes."

Martin filed a Notice of Appeal on September 24 at 4:30 p.m. - about 36
hours before Vignes was to face his execution. Noting the urgency of the
matter, the Court of Appeal duly scheduled a hearing for the following afternoon.

There was a healthy measure of judicial audacity in the simple filing of
a Notice of Appeal two days before an execution, as such a step had never
before been taken in Singapore. The court's response to this inventive tactic, scheduling the hearing for less than 24 hours later, was itself unprecedented.

Not overly hopeful of a favourable decision from the court on the following
day, R. Martin also sent another appeal to the official residence of the President of Singapore, SR Nathan, on the 24th. The following day, the President's
principle private secretary, Pek Beng Choon, sent a reply letter by courier
saying that s/he had been "directed to inform you that the decision of the
President as conveyed to the father of the prisoner in the letter dated 5 September 2003 (i.e., the dismissal of the clemency appeal) stands." Yet another
small door had been slammed shut. As unreceptive as the three-judge panel
that afternoon might prove, it could also well be the last chance for Vignes
Mourthi to remain alive past the following morning.

As R. Martin was getting ready to leave his home that Thursday morning, he lingered a bit longer before the photo of his mother, which stood on a small altar to her memory Martin had set up in his bedroom. She, and her death three years earlier, had inspired him to take on this near hopeless case. Could her spirit now give him an extra burst of energy and inspiration to pull this case out of the fire at the very last moment? Martin then finished dressing and headed off to his office. He knew already he would have a long, gruelling day ahead of him.

Those attracted to the notion of Pathetic Fallacy might have gazed up at the skies on the 25th of September and found a frightening omen for Vignes Mourthi and those close to him. By noon, a carpet of dark clouds had spread across the skies over Singapore; about 1:15, those clouds had opened and rain poured down in torrents upon the Lion City. Over at Changi Prison, the cloudburst did nothing to lift the spirits of the young man whose fate would be finally decided within a few hours.

Back in the Chinatown section, his lawyer peered out the window at the pelting rain and winced. He searched the sky for some sign of a let-up, but found none. Reflexively, he uttered, "Dammit!" Martin is not a strong believer in Pathetic Fallacy, but you can't discount such portents entirely. Not in a case in which the twists of Fate had played so strong a role up till then.

The final hearing started at 2:15 p.m., less than 16 hours before Vignes Mourthi's scheduled appointment with the hangman. As two o'clock approached, an overstressed Attorney Martin suddenly realised that he needed a quick wardrobe change. Not only had he been exhausting himself putting in 10 to 12-hour days for the past week, sometimes even 18 hours, but he had also been exhausting his supply of black-and-whites (black trousers, white shirt), the standard uniform for both advocates and judges in Singapore. Having been too busy to send his laundry to the cleaner's, Martin only realised early Thursday afternoon that he had no fresh white shirt or black trousers to wear to this most important hearing.

Conceding that seasoned attire would not make the best impression in court, Martin decided he had to rush out and buy a clean shirt and another pair of dark trousers. The easiest thing to do would be simply to pick up a new ensemble at the UOB shopping centre, a short hop from the court-house.

At 1:45 - or about 15 minutes before the scheduled start of the hearing - Martin quickly made his way to G2000, a popular men's shop there, where he snatched a decent-looking shirt and pair of trousers off the rack, then told the salespeople not to bag his purchase, as he intended to slip back into the fitting room and throw on the new shirt and trousers right then and there. Decked out in his fresh attire, Martin then hurried out of the shop and out to the side street where a friend was waiting for him in his car.

But the elements were still conspiring against the counsel. As he approached the street door, he was again greeted by sheets of lashing rain. Under these circumstances, a swim to the court might have been more appropriate than a ride. He looked down the street to where his friend's car was double-parked on the corner, across the street from the UOB centre. He made a mad dash for it. Though it was only a short sprint, Martin wasn't able to outrun the rain. He was pretty much soaked as he climbed into the car. This meant that Martin arrived at the heavily air-conditioned courtroom drenched, which did not help his mood any. Worse, this last-minute clothes run had broken his concentration a bit.

Vignes Mourthi, on the other hand, arrived at the courthouse dry. That's one of the few advantages of being a heavily guarded prisoner: you're whisked from a side door of the prison into a waiting van, taken to the courthouse where you're whisked out again, shepherded into a back entrance, then rushed upstairs via private lift to the floor where the hearing or trial is to take place. And, of course, you have three policemen with you the whole time - standing close, watching your every move. All of this heavy protection because two years earlier Vignes was carrying a bag with 27.65 grams of heroin stuffed into it.

For this final hearing, Vignes had arrived in court not only handcuffed, but also with manacles on his ankles. His demeanour now was more sombre than at the two previous hearings. He smiled at his lawyer, but one could see obvious strain behind that smile. There were creases of gloom at the corners of his eyes as the police officers helped him into the defendant's dock.

Martin looked back at him about five times during the proceedings, and each time, Vignes had a stoic expression etched into his face. It was almost as if, over the last week, he had reconciled himself to his fate.

All the family members from the earlier hearings were there as well - father, mother and all three sisters. Vignes' wife had come to none of these hearings, having remained back in her native Perak state with her family. The case had put an irredeemable strain on the marriage. She was totally dejected by the situation, was upset with her husband and the bonds of a short marriage. (Remember, the couple had been married only five months and one day at the time of his arrest). She had not even visited him a single time in Changi Prison.

The gallery at the courtroom was once more filled, again with many journalists and other lawyers increasingly curious as to how this case would turn out. Amongst the large gathering in the gallery were Martin's law friends as well as his secretary. Lincoln Teo, his lay assistant and good friend, was also in the upstairs gallery, sitting not far from the family. In fact, Teo's attention was focused more on the reactions of the family than on the actions of the three judges hearing this appeal. Journalists were packed into the spectator benches down below.

Martin speculates that most of the lawyers had ensconced themselves upstairs because of the controversial nature of the case; there was a fear of coming a little too close to this very touchy matter. And despite all those warm bodies, it was cold in the courtroom, though the rains had stopped by the time the judges took their seats on the bench.

The final appeal was heard before a three-judge panel headed up by Singapore's Chief Justice Yong Pung How. The other two justices on the panel were Judge of Appeal Chao Hick Tin and Justice Tan Lee Meng. As it turns out, two of these three justices, Chao Hick Tin and the Chief Justice himself, had sat on the coram which had dismissed the appeal arising from the original verdict back in January. Seeing a possible conflict of interest, Martin began the session by arguing that these two men should disqualify themselves, as only Justice Tan Lee Meng could be objective in the case. The other two would have to rule against their own earlier ruling if they were to grant a new trial or even a stay of execution. "I don't intend impudence, but I urge that Chao and Yong, who presided at the last hearing, be disqualified from the bench," Martin began his unusual request.

In fact, Martin devoted almost the first 45 minutes of his presentation to this request for a disqualification. The main thrust of his argument was two-fold: 1) that there should be not only no actual bias, but also no apparent bias overshadowing the hearing; and 2) that there shouldn't be any apparent bias in the mind of the public; that justice be seen to be done.

Citing the legal principle of nemo judex non causa sua, which states that you cannot be judged on your own cause, Martin argued that neither Chao nor Yong should be placed into the uncomfortable position of ruling against themselves from an earlier judgement.

Unfortunately, both Chief Justice Yong and JA Chao were the two permanent members of the Court of Appeal. At the end of Martin's plea, these two gentlemen joined their colleague Justice Tan in ruling that they could not be disqualified unless the applicant presented strong reasons showing that they would be unable to act objectively. Apparently, the fact that they would have to rule that they had made a grievous mistake some nine months earlier was not considered a strong enough reason. The two justices even pointed that this would not be the first time they had ruled on a final appeal that they themselves had earlier rejected. As the Chief Justice remarked to the defence counsel, "Your impressions of the law may be right, but they are not in accordance with mine."

It was once more Martin standing alone against the two big guns of the Attorney General's office, Bala Reddy and Francis Ng. The opposing sides knew each other's case well by now. This hearing lasted almost three hours, from its opening until the final decision. Martin was given some two hours and 15 minutes for his presentation, with very few interruptions during that time. The judges were obviously on best behaviour to give him the fairest hearing they could.

In fact, Chief Justice Yong is commonly known for his many interruptions, often with caustic remarks tossed at one or the other lawyer, though more often at each lawyer in turn. But there was none of that at this session, already overly charged with tension.

The main part of the appeal focused on two points. At one stage during Martin's submission, Justice Chao chastised the lawyer for repeating himself on some points. Martin immediately countered with his argument that as these points were so important, with a man's life literally hung in the balance, he needed to repeat them to register full impact.

The various parties also raised new issues at this hearing, such as the question of why and whether the Court of Appeal even had jurisdiction in a case such as this. A more significant new issue raised here, by Martin, was the fact that the informer Tahir was never produced, nor was any testimony from him ever submitted at the trial or subsequent appeals. How a central player in the whole drama should suddenly have disappeared from the stage at a crucial moment was a matter of some importance, Martin maintained.

About two hours into his presentation, the defence lawyer submitted a new document to the court saying that he had filed a constitutional reference on the issue of the informer. At this point, the Chief Justice did assert his authority and told the attorney that he should go ask the president to convene a constitutional court and argue this matter where it belongs, in front of them. With that, the present court had smacked down this key argument without even giving it consideration.

Martin refused to back down, however. He said that the court in session did, in fact, have the power to look at any constitutional questions and that in this case they should exercise that power. But the judges also stood firm in their positions on this issue.

Midway through his submission, the counsel noticed that the sky outside was again darkening, and began to suspect that maybe the elements were really on his side today. Martin had by chance readied a short but apt quote, and as another cloudburst began, he recited the opening of Portia's famous speech from the courtroom scene in Merchant of Venice. "The quality of mercy is not strain'd," he began. "It droppeth as the gentle rain from heaven upon the place beneath." Many of those in the courtroom looked out at the rain beating against the windows and laughed as Martin delivered that line. But the sharpest point he wanted to make came with the next line: "It is twice blest; it blesseth him that gives and him that takes." This speech was followed by a few rounds of muffled applause. After all, Shakespeare is rarely a bad place to turn for expert testimony.

Throughout the proceedings, Vignes' parents and three sisters watched with a mix of engrossment and bewilderment as their minimal command of English kept them from understanding much of what was going on. They were gesticulating vigorously, trying to communicate or ask help in keeping abreast of the developments down below. A couple of sympathetic policemen keeping watch in the gallery actually tried to comfort them at this stage.

About an hour later, as the impassioned defence lawyer was winding up his arguments, he turned towards his eminent adversary and asked whether "..the Deputy Public Prosecutor is still maintaining that an innocent man can be hanged due to procedural matters." Again, as he had in the second hearing, Bala Reddy refused to reply to this loaded question. But Martin did get a quick response from another quarter: the Chief Justice himself. Yong said, "Yes; the answer is yes."

Martin was numb with shock to hear such a pronouncement from so august a member of the Singapore legal establishment. He stood for a moment, almost dumb-founded, his jaw virtually frozen. Finally, he found the energy to utter his own reply to his question: "No; the answer is no. Article 9 (1) of the Constitution says 'No man shall be deprived of his life or liberty save in accordance with the law.' Law here means due process, which further means that an innocent man cannot be hanged, albeit it for want of procedure."

At around five o'clock, the Chief Justice made a unilateral decision, declaring that Martin's "eloquence and conscientiousness" presentation had "crystallised their (the three judges') thoughts" and there was no longer any need for the state's attorneys to respond to the defence arguments: they simply dismissed the appeal. (Martin later mentioned that he thought the Chief Justice's praise for his 'eloquence and consciousness' had a sarcastic tone to it.) Chief Justice Yong also pointed out that he had never before given an attorney the length of time to present his case that Martin had just enjoyed. Most lawyers at the appeal process are given a grace period of 20 minutes; Martin had received the better part of three hours.

But not even Shakespeare's eloquence had been able to sway the court. Today, there was no mercy to season pungent justice. After telling DPP Reddy that he didn't need to say anything more, the Chief Justice turned back to Martin and said, "You'd better say goodbye to your client. That's all you can do."

At the end of the hearing, a totally despondent Vignes Mourthi rose and addressed the bench through his interpreter. It was a spontaneous gesture, and even his own lawyer was taken aback that the defendant would make such a move. Vignes simply asked the Chief Justice why he was being executed. He said that he was not afraid to die, but if he was going to die the next morning, he wanted to know the reasons for his execution, why his energetic 32-point appeal had just been dismissed. The jurist's response to the man facing death the next morning was swollen with irony: he said the decision would be published in due course and everyone could find the reasons there.

The judges then rose and retired into their chambers. In doing so, they missed a fair amount of excitement unleashed in the courtroom they had just vacated. (Lincoln Teo later recalled the scene as being "near pandemonium".) From the gallery, the defendant's mother started screaming, then began banging her head against the wall. She was quickly restrained by two of her daughters before she could seriously injure herself.

In the meantime, Mourthi Vasu, the father, had leaned over the gallery railing and shouted down to his son, "Be strong. Go with strength." Poignantly, Vignes shouted back, "Don't worry, father!" Mr Vasu then turned and started to move quickly from the gallery down to the main floor of the courtroom, desperate to touch his son and speak to him once more at this most crucial moment.

A resisting Vignes was quickly dragged down the spiral staircase into the underground passage from which he would be escorted to the police van. Vignes looked at his lawyer sadly as the police detail started to remove him from the scene. Martin didn't really know what to say, but he scrabbled for some words of consolation. He called out loudly, "Don't worry, Jesus Christ and Goddess Mariamman, the Goddess of Mercy and Justice, will be with you." He wanted to add a more bracing sentiment, but all he could come up with was, "This is just a temporary exit. I hope you take care of yourself." Strangely, there were no tears in the condemned man's eyes.

Meanwhile, the father was still rushing, trying to get past the police to his son. But before the older man could get close enough, his condemned son had disappeared down the staircase. Was the back of his son's head going down those stairs the last view of Vignes alive that Mourthi Vasu was ever to have?

When the three sisters and mother had made their way down, they asked the lawyer what exactly was happening and what was going to happen next. Martin explained to them in Tamil all the main points of what had just transpired. Although his words were meant to be some form of solace, however feeble, they seemed to open a fresh wound within the mother, who again started banging her head against the wall. Again, the three daughters, heavily distressed themselves, pulled her away from the wall and took her in their arms. The father had a totally forlorn look on his face, as if he were about to lose not only his son, but all of his family. Caught up in the tumultuous emotions of the moment, Attorney Martin turned to a reporter from Singapore's New Paper and said, "I'm totally distraught. I don't think I can continue to practice law here in Singapore with dignity, fearlessness and a passion for justice." He then turned back to the family, to again offer whatever solace he still could.

After the turmoil in the courtroom had settled down, Mourthi Vasu rushed out to Changi Prison hoping to visit his son one last time. But as it was after five p.m. when he arrived at the prison gates, the father was refused permission to see his son. Regulations on visiting hours took precedence over one final goodbye.

Martin and his supporters then gathered in a hotel not far from the Supreme Court building for a press conference they had scheduled earlier - hoping then, of course, to be handling questions about their joyous triumph. As events turned out, there was little to do there but to rehash their basic arguments for a new trial and all that had just transpired. The mood was overwhelmingly sombre. Ex-attorney MG Guru, who had been too exhausted from his research and collating to attend the actual hearing, joined the rest of the team at this gathering and learned how all his hard work had apparently been for naught.

The press conference ended not with a bang, but a whimper: after the rich flood of words spoken in the last three weeks, what else remained to be said?

Formal Acknowledgement Given

On the 20th of September 2003, a letter signed by Peck Tiang Hock, superintendent of Changi Prison went out to Vignes' father, Mourthi A/L Vasu, notifying him that the death sentence imposed on his son was to be carried out less than a week later, on September 26. Mr Vasu was also informed that he and other family members could visit Vignes at the prison from 23 to 25 September.

The formal letter also advised Vignes' father to make all necessary funeral arrangements. If he were unable to do so, the letter announced, the state itself would carry out a cremation of Vignes' body. This, of course, ignored the deep significance of funerals in the Hindu religion. Though it's doubtful that the superintendent was at all aware of the family's strong religious beliefs.

At the foot of the letter from the prison superintendent was the motto of the prison system "Captains of Lives - Rehab - Renew - Restart". Across from this motto was "Singapore Quality Class", a seal which is a part of the Singapore government's programme to acknowledge and certify quality management. The prison system apparently qualified as 'quality management'.

The letter arrived at the JB address where Mourthi Vasu was staying with other family members. The family, of course, went to see the condemned man on all three days of special visitation rights. On these three days, the visiting hours were also extended - another clear sign of the prison's quality class.

Telegraphic Address: "DIRPRIS"
Telefax   : (65) 65469-208
CSMail Box : GVT 136
Mailbox Tel : (65) 65469-215

CHANGI PRISON
11 JALAN AWAN
SINGAPORE 499420

Tel No.   : (65) 65469-215

Email   : Tiang_Hock_Peck@pris.gov.sg

Your Ref   :

Our Ref   : CP/COND 836/02

Date   : 20 Sep 2003

Mr Mourthi A/L Vasu
No 16-A Jalan Bukit Cagar Satu
80300 Johor Bahru
Malaysia

Dear Sir

COND 836/02-   VIGNES S/O MOURTHI

      This is to inform you that the death sentence passed on Vignes S/O Mourthi will be carried out on 26 Sep 2003.

2.   You and other family members may visit him from 23 Sep 2003 to 25 Sep 2003.

3.   You are advised to make the necessary funeral arrangements. If you are unable to do so, cremation will be carried out by the state.

4.   For further information, please contact :

      Mr Tay Koon Cher or Mdm Lau Pey Ling
      Changi Prison
      11 Jalan Awan
      Singapore 499420
      Tel : 65469203/4
      Fax : 65469208

      Thank you.

PECK TIANG HOCK
SUPERINTENDENT
CHANGI PRISON

CAPTAINS OF LIVES
REHAB • RENEW • RESTART

SINGAPORE
QUALITY CLASS

This is the customary letter that families of condemned prisoners receive before the person is to be hanged. Vignes' version comes complete with the Prison Services slogan, "Captains of Lives". The slogan refers to a very recent softer, more rehabilitatory approach to all prison inmates BUT condemned prisoners. The irony of the slogan appears to have escaped the Prison Services.

117

Chapter 8

ANOTHER LAST CHANCE

In the struggle for existence, it is only on those who hang on for
ten minutes after all is hopeless, that hope begins to dawn.
- G.K. Chesterton

R. Martin first thought he would just head back to Sri Mariamman temple; he felt a need to pray now, as there seemed little else for him to do. But
instead, he returned directly to his office, arriving about 6 p.m. For some
strange reason, he still was not ready to give up the fight. He was joined there
by three friends, new and old. The newest of these friends was MG Guru, the
former lawyer who had come on board before the third hearing and helped
him prepare that final appeal for the case. The second friend was Ricky Sng,
who had driven him to the court earlier in the day. The third happened to
be his very close friend, Lincoln Teo. Martin felt at least a little better having
the three of them around. He clearly needed to be surrounded by friends at
that moment.

The mood, nevertheless, was tremendously gloomy. At the end of all that
work, worry, argumentation and pain, it certainly looked like the time had
come to just throw in the towel, admit they had done their best but had been
engaged in a losing cause right from the start. But they resisted this morose
temptation. Martin argued that they should make one last push to save the
life of Vignes Mourthi.

The first thing they did was to sit down together and draft a letter to
Singapore's President, each one contributing a bit to the proper phrasing and

balance of the plea. Satisfied with what they had, they faxed it to his official residence at 7 p.m. Around 8:30, there was a knock at the door, and there stood a middle-aged female, holding a rather wet umbrella in one hand and a small packet in the other. This women was a presidential staffer, come from the Istana to hand-deliver the president's reply. The head of state regretted that he was unable to help them: the decision would have to stand.

Martin then quickly drafted a reply to this presidential reply, which he sent via e-mail shortly after 9 p.m. In this letter, a longish plea to the president in his capacity as 'guardian of the Constitution of the Republic of Singapore', he implored him to reconsider the unusual situation and at least issue a stay of execution. This missive again ran through many of the arguments about the constitutional questions surrounding the impending execution of Vignes Mourthi. It especially emphasised Martin's conviction that it was unfair for Chief Justice Yong and Justice Chao to be sitting in judgement on this motion, as they would have been called upon to issue a judgement against their own earlier decision. Given this double-bind, Martin asked, could it really be claimed that his client had been given a fair hearing earlier that day. This plea was also made against the Chief Justice's remark that an innocent man may be hanged for procedural reasons.

The e-mail was CC'ed to the prime ministers and deputy prime ministers of Singapore and Malaysia, Singapore's Minister of Law and UN Secretary-General Kofi Annan, amongst others. The case, they all felt, had now taken on not just regional significance, but international import because of its human rights implications.

Still bushed from his dedicated work over the past few days, MG Guru decided to head back home shortly after they sent out the e-mail. The other three then sat back and waited for another response from the President's office. When no reply had come by 10:30 p.m., Martin decided to make a truly personal appeal: he would try to serve notice on the President himself. The three hopped into Lincoln Teo's car and sped off to the Istana, the official residence of the Singapore president. This was one last desperate attempt at a desperate solution. But as they say, desperate times call for desperate measures.

Martin himself had suggested this step, feeling that the president had perhaps not actually been presented with all the facts or the full human dimensions of the case when he was weighing the possibility of clemency. If that were so, then a heartfelt personal appeal might prove enough to swing things around even at the last moment. (Lincoln Teo later admitted that he felt they had little chance of success even with this bold move. He went along solely to show his solidarity with his old friend, now emotionally stretched to the limits.)

Not inappropriately, the Istana complex today sits adjacent to a large, multi-storey shopping mall, Plaza Singapura. Singaporeans love their shopping as much as they love their president and their food, which is also abundantly available in the area of the Istana.

The Istana (a Malay word meaning 'palace') is a sprawling estate with soft, rolling green hills and beautiful 19th century buildings. The largest of these buildings is the Singapore president's official residence. The whole complex is surrounded by a high fence and guards are on duty 7/24.

Having reached the Istana in good time, the trio drove right up to the front gates, but found them locked and unattended. They then swung around to the side entrance, which was still open. Again driving right up to the gates, they braced themselves for what could be the very last appeal in this arduous journey.

Martin and Lincoln climbed out of the car and strode up to the guard posts flanking the entrance, where they handed their letter to the guards on duty. Martin then asked the guards to sign one copy, acknowledging receipt of the letter. As with low-gear functionaries everywhere, the guards were at first reluctant simply to sign their names to something they were unfamiliar with. They were, in fact, confused as to why they had to acknowledge the simple fact that they had accepted the letter.

Attorney Martin gave them a quick crash course on legal rules involving delivery of articles and why it was important for them to acknowledge receipt. Finally, they did so, and assured the two visitors that the letter would be handed over to the president.

The pair then headed back to the car and climbed in. What now? They had hand-delivered their urgent appeal to the president's address. It was less than seven hours before the scheduled execution of Vignes. The night had a certain calm about it; the hectic rhythms of this high-energy city had died down considerably. Was there nothing else they could do?

The Istana

The Istana is the official residence of Singapore's President, where he receives and entertains state guests. Located in the centre of town along busy Orchard Road, the entire Domain, as the complex is called, sprawls over 100 acres.

The centrepiece building was de-signed by Major John Frederick Adolphus McNair and originally served as a residence for the British colonial governor. It was built by Indian convict labourers between 1867 and 1869. The Istana (which means 'palace' in Malay) was completed in 1869 and was known as Government House until Singapore attained self-rule in 1959.

The entire brickwork, exterior plastering and most of the flooring and interior work of Government House were carried out by Indian convict labour brought in from Bencoolen in Sumatra as the unskilled local coolies at that time (who earned 3 - 7 cents per day) were deemed incapable of carrying out the classical design Major McNair had fashioned.

The main Istana building perches on the top of a small hill. The structure today stands at 140 metres above sea level. It was once actually possible to see the Indonesian islands to the south and the hills of Johore to the north on a clear day from the Istana, before the ubiquitous skyscrapers of Singapore's Central Business District obscured the view completely.

Desperately thinking of what other alternatives remained, Martin suddenly lit on one more possibility. It was far-fetched, but it might just be the one that could save his client.

They sped off back to the courts, a ten to fifteen minute drive from the Istana. A member of the bar for seven years, Martin was well aware that the courts would have closed for the day at 5 p.m. or shortly thereafter, but he was hoping there might be duty registrars there to deal with late-night ship arrests. (An arrest of a ship or ship's owner after the vessel has travelled within the jurisdiction of Singapore.)

Martin was not, of course, on any maritime business: he wanted to find a registrar and get an injunction filed against the Director for Prisons, ordering him to delay the execution. The grounds: the hanging now appeared, to him as well as some others, to be a violation of the Singapore Constitution, especially in view of what the Chief Justice had said earlier - that an innocent man could be hanged for want of procedure. The idea of serving such an injunction was, indeed, audacious. Nothing like this had ever happened before in the history of the Republic.

Shortly before midnight, the three reached the City Hall complex. This time, Lincoln Teo waited in the car while Martin and Ricky headed to the formidable front doors of the building. There they were greeted by security guards on the other side. The questors asked the guards to kindly open the locked doors for them, as Martin needed to speak to a duty registrar. The guard didn't quite understand. Martin then informed them that he was an attorney and they had to open the doors for him so that he could see a registrar, even at this late hour.

One of the guards replied that he didn't really think there was any registrar on duty that evening, but Martin pleaded with him to check. The guard nodded, then ducked inside. A short time later, he returned and, amazingly, opened the doors for these unknown, late-night visitors. (Martin assumed that this guard had sought and received confirmation from the chief security officer that it was alright to admit them.)

Entering, Martin and Ricky Sng started wandering the darkened, dreary corridors of the court annex to Registrar 1 and Registrar 2, but the guard was right: they were unable to find a soul in either of these rooms.

They breathed deeply, as if they had finally reached the end of an arduous race. The long, tense day had finally ground to a halt. They decided to go home, and started walking back to the front door. They wanted to thank the guards again for letting them in.

If this had been a Hollywood film, they would have run into a duty registrar on their way back out. The registrar would have listened to their story and quickly issued an injunction. In another part of the island, the Director of Prisons would have read the injunction, thrown it onto his desk in frustration, then picked up the phone to order a stay.

Or the story would have ended half an hour earlier, back at the Istana. The President and First Lady would have been returning from some function, seen the other car parked near the side gates, and the President would have told his chauffeur to pull over. He would have rolled down his window and asked the two men standing there what the purpose of this unexpected visit was. As they told their story, the President would have...

Yes, that's how Hollywood would have scripted it. But despite the great influence Hollywood exercises on much of Singapore's popular culture, when it comes to happy endings in the judicial field, the Island Republic remains in many ways very, very far from Hollywood.

What really happened back in late September 2003 is that Lincoln Teo dropped his two friends off at their homes, then headed home himself. The soothing night sky settled over the island as on any other day. Across the island, people slept - or tried to sleep. There were no heroics, no last-minute qualms of conscience from anyone who could have changed the course of events here. Around 5:30, while it was still quite dark outside, two men, one-time friends, were taken from their detention cells to a special area in Changi Prison. Preparations were made for a rather grim procedure. At 6 o'clock, maybe an hour before sunrise, a noose was placed around Vignes Mourthi's neck, another around Mourthi Angappan's. Hoods were carefully eased over their heads. Two traps were released. Within a minute, at most, both men were dead.

No, this was not Hollywood; this particular story was scripted with the bitter ink of reality. People are not saved in the nick of time where reality and 'proper' judicial procedures rule. In those places, people do get executed

- even when there's still some possibility they might be innocent. Things go on from there. And don't really change a lot. No matter how hard some people might try to change them.

Death By Hanging - The Brutal Facts

The prisoner is weighed the day before the execution. Rehearsals are performed several days before the hanging takes place, using a sandbag of the same weight as the prisoner. This is to determine the length of 'drop' necessary to ensure a quick

death. The 'drop' is based on the prisoner's weight, to deliver 1260 foot-pounds of force to the neck. The prisoner's weight in pounds is divided into 1260 to arrive at the 'drop' in feet.

If the rope is too long, the prisoner could be decapitated.If the rope is too short, death by strangulation will result - that can take as long as 45 minutes. The rope is about 3/4-inch

(2 centimetres) to 1 and 1/4-inch (3 centimetres) in diameter and about 30 feet (900 centimetres) long. It would be boiled and stretched to eliminate springing or coiling. The knot is lubricated with wax or soap - to ensure a smooth sliding action.

Immediately before the execution, the prisoner's hands and legs are tied and secured, the noose is placed around the neck, with the knot behind the left ear. A white hood is then pulled over the prisoner's head.

Hooding the prisoner saves the officials who have to witness the execution from seeing the prisoner's face as he is about to die and after the death. Not looking at the condemned person's face is one way of coming to terms with state-sanctioned murder, but righteousness is another.

The execution takes place when a trap-door is opened and the prisoner falls through. At the end of the 'drop' the body, still accelerating under the force of gravity, delivers a massive blow to the back and one side of the neck, which combined with the downward momentum of the body, breaks the neck and ruptures the spinal cord. The prisoner's weight causes a rapid fracture-dislocation of the neck.

Death by hanging is supposedly caused by dislocation of the third and fourth cervical vertebrae or as-phyxiation. However, instantaneous death is rarely achieved. Death by hanging is not a humane method of exterminating a healthy human being. It is a very brutal and cruel death.

The condemned often collapse or faint before the noose can be properly positioned over his head. Death by hanging is often botched, or carried out in such a way as to intentionally maximise the prisoner's suffering.

Botched hangings that occur within prisons are not reported. Botched hangings result in strangulation, obstructed blood flow, or beheading. If the prisoner has strong neck muscles, is of light-weight, if the 'drop' is too short, or if the noose is wrongly positioned, the fracture-dislocation will not be rapid and death results from slow asphyxiation. The prisoner writhes and throttles to death over several minutes. In medical terms - death from cerebral contusion, shock and asphysia.

There have been reported cases of the rope breaking during the 'drop', which resulted in the prisoner falling to the ground. After officials replaced the broken rope, the prisoner would again have to endure the emotional and physical torture of being hanged for a second time, usually taking place within the hour.

In another reported incident, the head of a prisoner split from the body during the hanging.

When a human being is hanged, his face becomes engorged, the tongue protrudes, the mouth vomits and drools, the eyes pop, the body defecates, violent movements of body limbs occur, and the face begins to turn a greyish-black. Although the prisoner may appear to be unconscious, the heart does not completely stop beating for some 20 minutes.

Most people do not know that a human heart beats on its own -and continues to do so - even when the rest of the body has shut down. This happens because the human heart is hard-wired with electrical impulses. Thus, during a phase of some 20 minutes, the pulsations of the doomed heart become fainter and slower as the heart struggles to maintain its normal function to pump blood throughout the body, intent on keeping the body alive. Eventually, the heart lapses into a spasmodic rhythm, then begins to flutter, before it slowly collapses, fails, and finally stops all movement.

In medical terms - this is the "true" time of death. The "official" time of death portrayed to the public is deliberately distorted for the obvious reason - to brainwash the public into believing that hanging is clean and quick.

It has been generally assumed that fracture-dislocation of the neck causes instantaneous loss of sensation. Sensory pathways from below the neck may rupture, but the sensory signals from the skin above the noose and from the trigeminal nerve may continue to reach the brain until hypoxia blocks them.

Chapter 9

RITES AND DUTIES

Sometimes you just need someone there to hold your hand.

It had been pretty much a restless night for all those closely involved in the Vignes Mourthi case. MG Guru, who had come in late but provided valuable assistance in the end-spurt legal preparations, got little sleep, then rose early, before 6 a.m. to recite his morning prayers. He prayed especially on this day to the Hindu god Vinayaka, also known as Ganesh, revered as the god of benevolence. When he finished, it was just after 6 a.m. Guru assumed he would soon hear from R. Martin on the next stage of activities.

Martin himself returned home about 12:30 a.m., thoroughly exhausted but with little hope for a sound night's sleep. He sorely needed his sleep, however, as he had another case scheduled for early in the morning. But for the next three and a half hours, Martin lay tossing and turning, thinking not only about the case that was now closed but what lay ahead for all those involved.

The thoughts that coursed most intensely in the lawyer's head were of what Vignes Mourthi himself must have been thinking during those last hours. He was also deeply concerned about Vignes' family. He knew that the parents would now have to make rushed funeral arrangements, even though they were so ill-equipped for this task. How were they going to handle these arrangements, along with the emotional trauma of the execution? Realising that these were poorly educated people dealing with another country's complicated rules, regulations and practices - and now caught in a maelstrom of hectic activity to work through these rules and practices - Martin knew that the family would need some heavy-duty assistance. The next stage would perhaps be even more difficult than what they had just gone though.

On a deeper level, the young lawyer empathised with the pre-execution grieving process they must be struggling with right then. Having engaged himself with this matter even before taking on the Vignes' case, he had discovered that the most trying part of the grieving process connected to the death penalty actually came before the loved one was dead. It is in these last hours that those close to the condemned fully realise that this is a death that could be averted - but it won't be. At best, this could be termed as a man-made disaster.

Martin finally managed to fall asleep around 4 a.m. But he in no way made up for the sleep debt he'd been accumulating over the previous ten days. While he usually rises about 7:30 on a workday, that morning some mechanism deep within worked like an internal alarm clock to wake him at precisely 6 a.m. He breathed heavily as he sat up. Though a comfortable distance from Changi Prison, he could somehow sense what was happening there at that hour. Shortly after waking, Martin looked out the window at the slate-grey sky and said to himself, "Oh, my God - he's gone, he's gone." And there was really nothing more to say at that point.

We have no accounts of how Vignes Mourthi and Moorthy Angappan spent that last night, in separate cells barely ten metres apart. Neither was around much after 6 a.m. to report on how the night had gone and nobody who saw them in their last twenty minutes alive seems to have asked them if they had slept well. We can only assume that it was not the most peaceful of nights for either man.

The weather that morning of 26 September was quite sunny and would remain so for the entire day. What Pathetic Fallacy reading could one take from that? Perhaps this was a signal to start a new chapter. Attorney Martin certainly knew he now had to turn the page, get on with his career. This case was, in many ways, a caesura in the usual work of his legal practice. And yet it had swallowed so much of his time and energy.

As he started to get ready for his workday, Martin again gazed at the picture of his mother where it sat on the special altar in his room. By great coincidence, this very day was the third anniversary of her death, according to the Hindu calendar. He tried to gain some strength from this fact and all the things that she had taught him about the sanctity of life and the importance of standing by one's beliefs. And above all, compassion for the poor and downtrodden.

Martin arrived at court for his early hearing shortly before 9 a.m. This case was a minor criminal infraction. There were no impassioned speeches, no wrangling with recalcitrant judges over matters of constitutional jurisdiction, no appeals to mercy. This session drew to a calm finish sometime after 10 am.

As Martin was walking out from the courtroom, he switched his mobile phone back on; it started ringing almost immediately. When he answered, there was a shrill cry at the other end. This was Sangari, the younger sister of Vignes. Highly distraught, she struggled to get out the words between spasms of crying. Finally, she managed to tell Martin that her brother was now dead and that the family, who had been at the prison since 7 a.m., had been informed by prison authorities that they had to collect the body from the prison sometime between 11 a.m. and 1 p.m. If the body remained uncollected past that time, Sangari moaned, the state would proceed with its own cremation.

Of course, the family had been warned about this possibility five days earlier in that aseptic letter from the Superintendent of Prisons. However, under such emotional duress, they had failed to make any funeral arrangements. Now it looked as if the state might carry out a cremation stripped of any warmth, ceremony or emotion. If one can imagine something like a cold cremation, that's what lay ahead for Vignes' body.

When the family was given the 1 pm. deadline on the morning of the 26th, they began pleading with the authorities at the prison not to consign the body to state cremation as they were from Malaysia and needed more time to arrange for relatives and friends to come down. Moreover, they had no money for a funeral at that moment, nor did they know how to actually go about arranging for the funeral. All those things that R. Martin had worried about hours earlier as he lay tossing and turning in bed had come to pass.

Martin told the sister that he found that 1 pm. deadline ridiculous. The police, he went on, should be a little more sensitive to the family's dilemma at such a trying time. Also, Martin pointed out that the bloodless letter the family had received about the execution failed to mention any cut-off time for collecting the body. He felt it not only insensitive but grossly unfair to inform the family only now about such a deadline.

Despite the family's pleas for some flexibility, the prison officials told them in no uncertain terms that the body had to be collected by 1 pm. at the latest or it would be disposed of in the state's way. Martin told Sangari to calm down; he would see to it that proper funeral arrangements were made.

Immediately after hanging up on Sangari Mourthi, Martin called a Buddhist casket company and asked them to carry out the funeral arrangements. He then directed them to go to Changi Prison immediately and collect the body. He also stressed that he would pay for all the funeral services they provided.

But why a Buddhist rather than a Hindu funeral home? Martin had contacted the former because he realised that the body would need to be embalmed if the funeral were to be delayed. In Hindu practice, the corpse is usually cremated within 48 hours of death, so embalming is an art almost no Hindu funeral homes in the Lion City have mastered.

(Chinese Buddhists, Taoists and Christians in Singapore all typically have week-long wakes, allowing friends, relatives and business associates to drop by at their convenience and see the deceased and the survivors. Embalming is thus essential for these groups, especially in a tropical climate such as Singapore's.)

But before hanging up, Martin was gripped by a second thought: he told the funeral hearse to come directly to the Subordinate Court, meet him there and then proceed on to Changi. Martin wanted to be able to give them full instructions and then follow them in a taxi to the prison. (The cab of the funeral company's van only had room for two people. The rear of the van was generally reserved for those who had given up the habit of breathing.)

The funeral home van arrived about 15 minutes later. Martin clarified the situation with the two men in the van, hopped into a waiting taxi, and they were all off to Changi.

This two-vehicle convoy had just pulled off the expressway and was about a ten-minute drive from the prison when Martin received another phone call from Vignes' sister with a new jolting surprise: the body was no longer at Changi Prison. It had been collected a short time before and taken to Mount Vernon Crematorium for cremation. It seems that the prison authorities could not even wait for their own 1 p.m. deadline: they had made official funeral arrangements and released the body to Rajoo Casket, a respected Hindu funeral home. And even though it was only a little after 11 o'clock, the

Mourthi family were told that the cremation could proceed at any time now. Understandably, they were in near-panic mode.

Martin quickly grabbed his mobile, rang the people in the funeral van, asked them to pull over, informed them of the turn of events, and then the van and taxi simply spun a U-turn and raced off to Mount Vernon Crematorium in the Upper Aljunied section of the island, hoping to beat the flames.

About 20 minutes later, the van and taxi pulled up to the front of the crematorium. Luckily, the funeral hearse from Rajoo Casket was sitting there with Vignes' body still within. Martin jumped out of the taxi and went over to assess the situation.

It was not by any means the easiest of situations to assess. Vignes' mother had meanwhile jumped onto the hearse belonging to the Hindu funeral home and started beating her son's chest as vigorously as she could, in a frenzied attempt to revive him. Herself in something like high hysteria, she apparently believed that Vignes was in a state of shock or trauma from the hanging and not really dead yet. She was still not ready to accept that her only son was gone. The other people present - her four family members and the workers from Rajoo Casket - just stood there watching her. They realised that it would not be too wise to try to restrain her at this moment.

She had evidently been working frenetically to revive Vignes for ten to fifteen minutes when Martin arrived. She pounded on the chest a bit longer, before looking up to see that Martin had joined the group. She pointed to the corpse and started crying to the lawyer, "Look at what has happened to my son, look at what they've done to him. Look at the cut."

Martin approached gingerly: he had never before seen an executed man. His first viewing of such had to be a young man whose life he himself was fighting to save less than 24 hours earlier. Being a member of the bar, Martin had often heard from colleagues what an execution entails and what injuries a hanged man incurs. However, the appearance of this young man was unlike anything he had expected to see. An extremely deep cut ran as far around the neck as Martin could see. This sight shocked even the jaded lawyer. He felt nausea overtaking him and had to brace himself. He asked himself how human beings could be so cruel as to do such a thing to a fellow human being, even one deemed to be a criminal.

Martin turned to the man from Rajoo Casket, who supposedly had some experience in these matters, and blurted out, "Did they behead him or what?" Of course, the head was not detached from the body, but the lacerations made by the rope were indeed deep enough to suggest that only a little more slicing was necessary to sever the head completely. (The depth of the lacerations strongly suggest that the execution team had overestimated Vignes' body weight in preparing the drop; see Box Text)

This was not the only shock: there were still dark patches of dried blood staining the white T-shirt from where it had oozed from the neck. More horrifically, one could still clearly smell the blood.

There then followed a rather charged discussion between the lawyer and the Rajoo Casket people, which included Mr Rajoo, owner of the firm. The men from the funeral parlour said that they were there to cremate the body, that's what they had been commissioned to do by someone close to the family, and they intended to do it. Speaking to them in Tamil, Martin explained that he had engaged the Buddhist funeral home to take charge of the whole affair, and that he and the entire family wanted to call off the impending cremation. He further explained that they needed to postpone the ceremony for a few days so that friends and family could journey down from Malaysia and that it was therefore necessary to embalm the body.

Martin then appealed to the basic decency of the two men from Rajoo: he told them that all anyone could do at this point was to grant the deceased and the family the respect connected to a proper funeral. He also mentioned something that Mourthi Vasu had confided to him: that shortly before his death, his son had put a curse upon the nation of Singapore. It was a mild curse, however, one that only asked that Singapore would be accountable for this 'miscarriage of justice' inflicted upon him (in his view). For that reason, he wish to be cremated here so that this "miscarriage of justice should be noted". However, after the cremation had taken place on Singapore soil, Vignes wished to have his ashes returned to his native Malaysia. This return to native soil was, in fact, the more important part of his request. But the family was now worried that the Singapore authorities might take the body elsewhere and dispose of it.

After considering Martin's arguments for a few moments, the two men from Rajoo agreed to see if they could come to an arrangement satisfactory to all the parties now involved.

Martin nodded, then made his way to the main desk at the crematory and notified the clerk there that the impending cremation of the recently executed man had to be postponed. He asked what the next available dates for cremation were. The crematory official took him into his cool gaze for a moment, then told him that their schedule was entirely booked for the whole weekend. Martin then inquired about Monday or Tuesday of the upcoming week, to which he answered that it was hard to say at that time. The gentleman was obviously not pleased with the postponement and the loss slot that it had created.

Martin found these responses not satisfactory and told the Mount Vernon clerk as much. "you seem to have a lot of advance bookings for Hindu funerals there. You really seem to know when people are going to die, and have made advance arrangements accordingly." He then told the crematory employee that if they could not give him an appointment within the next few days, he would see that the body was embalmed for the maximum time, which would mean a headache for them.

Headache in what way, the clerk asked. Martin replied that he would certainly let the press know about this matter if they couldn't come up with an early alternative date. Every day that the body lay there waiting for its final send-off, more public attention would be aroused via the media. And it would certainly not be good publicity for Mount Vernon if more and more people came to hear about this whole unfortunate episode.

At this, the man from the crematory threw another glance at their calendar and suddenly discovered that both Monday and Tuesday would be fine for the rescheduled cremation. In fact, they could even squeeze them in on Saturday or Sunday, if necessary.

The attorney then quickly stepped outside again where Vignes' parents and sisters were still gathered around the van bearing his body. Upon conferring quickly with the family, Martin determined that early Monday evening would probably be the best time for the funeral. This would allow family and friends from northern Malaysia to make their way down and pay their last respects, but would not defer the final rites too long. (Hindus do not believe in keeping the body too long after death.) Settled: the Mount Vernon schedulers and Martin set Monday for the cremation.

It remained only to strike some agreement between the family, Rajoo Casket, and the Buddhist funeral home. Actually, those two companies had been discussing just this matter while Martin was trying to reschedule the cremation. Mr Rajoo pointed out that his firm would be best for conducting all the funeral arrangements in the Hindu manner. They could arrange with the Buddhist company to do the embalming and hold the wake, but they wanted to keep the final funeral ceremonies in their hands. The Buddhist funeral parlour was clearly amenable to this division of labour. And although he had a cash flow problem during that time (four weeks of intensive pro bono work had severely drained his finances), Martin was committed to covering the funeral expenses himself. He knew well that a proper funeral was beyond the means of the Vasu family, especially after all the debts they had accumulated recently.

Despite his low cash stock, Martin told the man from Rajoo Casket that he wanted the best possible funeral for Vignes and even slipped him $1,000 in cash right there as down payment on getting the best treatment for the deceased. (The funeral eventually wound up costing just over $7,000 for everything, divided between the two funeral homes.)

Agreement reached, the body was then turned over to the Buddhist firm, who took it away for the embalming process. One major hurdle in getting a proper funeral had been overcome. The body was then laid out for a public wake at the Chinese funeral home on Bright Hill Road in the Bishan section of Singapore.

Actually, very few Singaporeans turned up for the wake, even though it ran for three full days. Martin and some others believe that the low turnout by locals was due to various shades of fear as well as the public stigma attached to attending something as controversial as this.

However, on Sunday, there was a rather heartening visit to Bright Hill by one Singaporean woman. This particular lady knew neither the defence team nor anyone in the family. After paying her respects, she approached R. Martin and told him why she had come. She had read about the case in the papers, she related, and was quite moved by the whole story. She told herself that she had to do something, however small, to show her displeasure at the possible injustice surrounding the case. She had even asked some of her friends to attend the wake, but they were all frightened of being seen there. She was herself frightened, she admitted, and was told insistently by these friends not to go. What if...?

Yes, what if. But that question could be turned around in different ways. This woman, herself an ethnic Indian, said that she had then prayed and asked guidance as to what she should do. Finally, she decided it was her duty as a caring human being to come and add whatever solace and support she could to the family and friends. She even donated some money to the family to help them deal with the funeral and other expenses. Martin was quite pleased to hear her account and to realise that their message was getting through clearly to some Singaporeans.

MG Guru came to the wake every day, staying for up to three hours each time, providing support to the family and encouragement to Martin. Martin's old and dear friend Lincoln Teo also turned up on Friday night and stayed for close to three hours, lending much appreciated support. He dropped in again on Sunday, but could only stay one hour on that visit.

One person who, strangely, did not turn up for either wake or funeral was Pushpa, Vignes' wife. She apparently felt herself so estranged from her husband, his family and their grief that she could not make the (admittedly) longish trip down to show a final act or love or affection. This was another blow to Vignes' family.

The lawyer himself stayed beside the family the entire three days, right there at the funeral home, never leaving until after the funeral itself. There were nine of them altogether by this time - Vignes' parents and three sisters, three of the dead man's friends from Malaysia, and Martin. They slept right under the coffin, on bags thrown onto the floor or on a couch nearby. They covered themselves with dhotis as they slept. Or tried to sleep. On Saturday, Martin was unable to catch any sleep at all.

Again, Vignes' mother was wailing over and over during these last three days, trying to kiss him every time she came close to the body. She also asked him again to talk to her as if, even now at this final stage, she could not accept that he was truly gone. The three sisters stood there looking at their brother with disbelief etched into their faces. They knew he was dead, but it was a knowledge that had not yet seeped fully into their hearts.

Because he chose to spend the time completely with Vignes' family, Martin had actually missed the anniversary prayers for his own mother. This was the first time since her death that he had failed to participate in the anniversary prayer ceremony, a fact which affected him emotionally. However, he sensed that on this one day his mother would have wanted him to be with this family in distress.

The three sisters and Martin would go out from time to time to buy food for the group at a nearby Indian take-away stall. Although most of those keeping the death watch had no real appetite during this sad weekend, food was always there for them when they needed it.

Curiously, Vignes' wife Pushpa never came to either the wake nor the funeral. She was back living with family in northern Malaysia, but so were many of the friends and relatives of the dead man who had made their way there. Apparently, the arrest, trial and conviction had severed all the emotional commitments she had to her husband. (Admittedly, she had only known this husband as a free man for five months.)

On Monday morning, the people from Rajoo Casket came by. They had even arranged for two Hindu priests to come along and perform all the religious rites connected to the funeral. This was a bonus: generally, it is only very wealthy Hindus who can afford to have priests come and perform the funeral rites. (The priests were attached to the Sri Siva Krishna temple in Woodlands.) By the start of the funeral ceremony, another ten relatives had arrived from Malaysia to take part and lend some numbers to the mourners.

His little niece told everyone that when she approached the body, her uncle Vignes opened his eyes and looked at her. The other members of her family realised that she was just playing a child's game, not too appropriate for the occasion.

By about three o'clock, the body was taken and ritually washed, the head was anointed with oil, then the deceased was dressed in a Western suit and shirt, complete with tie. This was also unusual for Hindu funerals, where the diseased are usually decked out in traditional Indian dress. But the family had apparently decided that they wanted something special, different for this ceremony. This death was itself different, after all. These rituals having been taken care of, the body of Vignes was placed back in the coffin and decked with flowers.

Martin had earlier given his secretary instructions to cancel all his appointments for that Monday. (Fortunately, he had no scheduled court hearings anytime that week.) He knew that he would be busy the whole day, either at the Bright Hill home or at Mount Vernon, seeing to the smooth operation of the funeral arrangements and looking after the family.

At the end, about 30 to 40 people showed up at Mount Vernon crematory for the final farewell. Martin had also taken a leading hand in arranging the final ceremony at the crematorium. He had brought along his favourite devotional CD's from various saints and seers of India. In addition, he had put up about 15 to 20 crucifixes around the room, along with a picture of Blessed Mary, mother of Jesus, reflecting Hindu reverence for all the religions. The hall had taken on a real ecumenical flavour, enhanced by the pictures of the 18 Siddhas pasted around the hall. The Siddhas were essentially Yogis who were also men of science and who supposedly founded the basis of Tamil medicine, and cosmicization of the human body through Yoga and Compassion.

Minor Matters

On a BBC HARDtalk interview which took place in September 2003 (and was televised on 23 September 2003), then Prime Minister Goh Chok Tong of Singapore was asked how many executions the city-state had carried out that year. The Prime Minister answered that he believed the number was "in the region of 70 or 80". When pressed as to why he couldn't be more exact, the PM replied, "I've got more important things to worry about."

Actually, the Prime Minister's estimate was wildly overdrawn. In fact, two days later, his office retracted the statement, announcing that capital punishment had been adminis-

tered only ten times so far that year. This figure itself may have been low, but it was much closer to the facts than the 70 or 80 hangings to which Prime Minister Goh had alluded.

It was clear that Mr Goh was not trying to cover up or play down the extent of state-ordered executions in the Lion City, as his guesstimate multiplied the actual figure many times. He was simply caught uninformed about the actual situation when served up this hardball question.

But what are we to make of the Prime Minister's explanation that he had "more important things to worry about"? Was this just a lame excuse? Probably not. The fact is, for well over a decade, in Singapore the main business of government has been business. The PAP-led government that has been running the tiny republic since self-government in 1959 mainly busies itself with keeping the economy humming along as smoothly as possible. Government ministers devote most of their energies to enticing investment into the thriving state and keeping employment up as high as the free market system and its vagaries allow. Top government officials also keenly pursue strong and friendly relationships with all those nations that seem likely to keep investment monies flowing into Singapore.

Something like executions of convicted felons is a minor matter for the government, certainly nothing to trouble the Prime Minister with. In fact, one reason why the question of capital punishment and all its parameters does not get examined more thoroughly by the authorities is probably that it is simply not considered that important.

So why do those jurisdictions that still employ hanging rely on this centuries-old method? In the case of Singapore, it's largely because they inherited this method from the British. Here, as in certain other areas, Singaporeans still maintain a respect for tradition!

Martin had also brought along 500 small, pin-on hearts which lit up around the edges for the ceremony. (He had had to dig into his pockets for an additional $1,500 in purchasing these hearts.) Originally intended for a wide-scale save-the-life-of-Vignes-Mourthi campaign that never quite got off the ground, these hearts were distributed by Martin to the thirty plus people who had come to the cremation and final ceremonies.

As the ceremony culminated, a small group of those closest to the deceased walked around the coffin three times, sprinkling water from a ceramic pot onto the corpse. This ritual symbolises the survivors' final leave-taking from the corporeal existence of the departed.

The pot itself is usually carried and then broken by the eldest son. As Vignes himself had no children, it would usually have fallen upon his father to perform this role in the ritual. But Mourthi Vasu was so weakened from the ordeal that he doubted he could carry the pot or properly break it, so the family asked R. Martin had to perform this necessary function in the final rites.

Finally, the procession around the coffin ended, the pot was broken and the body consigned to the flames. Vignes' mother started screaming as the coffin slid along

Hang It All

Hanging is presently used as a form of execution in 58 countries, including Singapore. One of those 58 countries is the United States, though hanging is employed in only three of the 38 states that still permit executions - Montana, New Hampshire and Washington state. (Not to be confused with Washington, D.C., which has abolished the death penalty.) But even those three states which have retained the hangman's noose also have the option of executing convicted criminals by lethal injection, the dominant form of execution in the United States today.

the belt to the incinerator. The doors closed on the coffin before the actual incineration began. It was similar to the final scene in the courtroom where Vignes had disappeared down the spiral staircase before the family could approach him: they just caught a last, fleeting glimpse of their son, their brother, their cousin, their friend.

After the body had disappeared behind the doors of the incinerator, various family members continued crying, clutching each other and shaking their heads in a mixture of grief and disbelief. They stood or sat in the cremation hall and did not want to leave. Finally, Mount Vernon employee approached and told them they had to leave. They had given until 7 p.m., standard closing time, for the funeral, and it was already 7:15. Could they please leave now as quickly as possible, the man asked politely. However, several family members remained too distraught to even take note of this request.

Attorney Martin decided that he had to take some action once more. He moved to the side and again put on the devotional music. This calmed most of the mourners down considerably. Slowly, they moved in small groups towards the exit. There was really nothing holding them there any more.

In the adjoining parking lot, the family climbed into a relative's van, as did Martin. They dropped Martin off a short time later and then drove back to Johor Bahru, Malaysia. Another chapter in the story had come to an end.

Three or four days later, an appointment was arranged for the next-of-kin to come and collect the ashes, now stuffed into an urn. Mourthi Vasu came down to the Mount Vernon crematorium to take his son back to Malaysia one last time. Those encouraging words that Vignes had uttered a number of times during the past three weeks - "Papa, I am coming home." - must have echoed poignantly in the father's head at this point. He was, indeed, coming back home.

The ashes were then scattered into the sea. Vignes Mourthy had come home.

Chapter 10

CLEARING THE PAPERWORK

The pursuit of truth shall set you free—even if you never catch up with it.

- Clarence Darrow

In mid-October, roughly three weeks after the execution, the Court of Appeal did release its reasons for having denied that final appeal one day before the execution. Once a criminal appeal has been dealt with, the court wrote, neither the Court of Appeal nor the High Court can re-open the case. Chief Justice Yong cited three precedents in rendering this decision. In one of these cases, Lim Choon Chye vs. Public Prosecutor, the appeal was dismissed even though the applicant asserted that fresh evidence proving innocence had turned up since the earlier denial of an appeal.

In this case, the former Judge of Appeal, M. Karthiegesu, had stated that it was not the Singapore parliament's intention to allow appellants an "indefinitely extended right of appeal". Therefore, a second appeal could not be allowed in any case where an appeal had already been heard and dismissed. Even if that case involved the death penalty and an irreversible error may have been made.

The 13th of October 2003 decision of the court was fairly short and sweet, written in clear and compelling language. It can only be hoped that on the day of its release, Vignes Mourthi, wherever he was, could finally appreciate the reasons why he was hanged, especially when he had personally made that request to see the written judgement.

Hanging Time: A Short History of the Noose

Today, hanging ranks as the second most common form of execution throughout the world, trailing only execution by gunfire. It is used as the primary or sole means of execution in Japan, Singapore, Malaysia, South Korea, India, Pakistan, Bangladesh, several African countries, including Botswana and Zimbabwe, and Middle Eastern lands such as Iran, Syria, Egypt, Jordan, Kuwait and Lebanon. It is also used in those Caribbean states which have retained the death penalty.

While the statistics are not complete (many countries do not issue full reports on the executions they carry out), it is known that in 2002, at least 115 men and 5 women were hanged around the world, with that count down to 99 men and 1 woman the following year. However, in 2004, there was another upward surge with at least 150 men and 7 women hanged. It is generally accepted that hang-ing as a form of execution originated in the Persian Empire around 2,500 years ago. It is prominently mentioned in the Bible, in the Book of Esther, where Hamman, a top advisor to the Persian king, had plotted to have Esther's uncle Mordechai hanged and all the Jews in the kingdom massacred. Esther, one of the king's wives, managed to convince her husband of Hamman's nefariousness and the monarch reversed the sentence and had Hamman and his ten sons hanged on the gibbet he had prepared for Mordechai.

Hanging of criminal offenders and defeated enemies is mentioned several times in earlier portions of the Bible, but it is believed that these victims were first either strangled or killed in battle and then hanged by the ancient Hebrews as a display of what happens to those who fall into disfavour. The practice is believed to have arrived in England with the Saxon invasion around 450 of the Modern Era. However, for many centuries, hanging remained the death penalty for more humble criminals. For instance, up through the end of the feudal period, peasants were typically hanged while the nobility enjoyed the quicker death of beheading.

Hanging quickly spread, and soon became a popular form of execution (indeed, the most popular until the early 20th century) throughout the world for two main reasons. Firstly, it was relatively cheap, in that all you needed was a sturdy rope, a place from which to hang that rope (in the earliest days, a simple tree trunk generally served that purpose), and a mobile platform on which to first stand the victim. The platform is then removed suddenly, causing strangulation or a broken neck to occur. In the meanest of circumstances, a chair or table would suffice for that platform.

Secondly, hanging made for a powerful public spectacle. The condemned persons were displayed above eye level, making them an accessible and arresting sight for any large crowd gathered around - or just passing by. Also, while there was a short period of obvious suffering involved, hanging did avoid the blood and gore of other execution methods, such as beheading, breaking on the wheel, drawing and quartering or burning. Various authorities thus thought that hanging served the cause of deterrence quite nicely: the victim could hang there in mid-air as a cautionary lesson but was unlikely to cause undue disgust or public revulsion.

Moreover, the hanged criminal could provide that cautionary lesson for quite a while. For many centuries, it was deemed good policy to allow executed miscreants to hang as long as they could, often until birds and other wild animals had picked the bones clean. With that method, people could choose to come to the hanging district (usually located just outside or at the edge of town) at will and observe the results of the punishment. Many *adults often brought along children to make sure the kids got whatever lesson their elders wished to impart.*

That's why hanging was for many centuries very much a gender-specific mode of execution. Females in the Persian Empire were strangled and not displayed. Centuries later, in medieval and early Modern Period German cities such as Frankfurt, many male criminals were hanged and left hanging while females were placed in a bag with heavy stones, then cast into a river or lake to drown. The fact is, birds and dogs would first tear off the clothing of a hanged corpse, meaning that within a few days, passersby were treated to the sight of naked bodies dangling in the breeze. In the interests of decency, females were thus excluded from this treatment.

As the Enlightenment took hold in many parts of Europe and the world, the long-term display of hanging victims was abandoned. Friends or relatives of hanged convicts were allowed to claim the bodies soon after death was officially declared. When neither of these came forward, the state would assume responsibility for taking down the body and providing it with a pauper's burial (usually in a mass grave). This change meant that convicted females could be hanged alongside their male counterparts.

However, as humanistic values in step with public disgust at the sight of hanging increased during the Modern Era, execution as a form of public entertainment was abolished and executions were henceforth moved inside prison walls. (Britain itself abolished public executions in 1868.) In Singapore, for instance, no members of the public (including immediate family members) are even allowed to attend the executions. In the Lion City, hanging as a vehicle of deterrence is to be achieved through word of mouth and written reports rather than direct experience of the public.

Chapter 11

A NATIONAL HERO BROUGHT LOW

Thou shalt not be a victim. Thou shalt not be a perpetrator.
Above all, thou shalt not be a bystander.
- Holocaust museum, Washington

Immediately following the Vignes Mourthi case, Attorney R. Martin found himself somewhat depleted - emotionally, physically... and financially. In addition to the time and energy he had devoted to the case (without receiving any financial compensation), Martin also saw some of his long-time, very well-paying clients drop him as their solicitor because they feared that he was now viewed as 'an anti-establishment figure' who would reflect negatively on them if he continued as their counsel. One local daily, The New Paper, reported: "Corporate Clients Drop 'Rude' Lawyer". This adverse publicity turned away even more clients.

Martin's preparations for the Hindu fire-walking ceremony, Thimithi, which took place in late October that year, helped him fill up again emotionally, spiritually and even physically. For his financial health, he swung back to those areas of the law which paid well, and at which he was already quite adept - civil litigation and intellectual property matters. The Vignes Mourthi case would stand as an emotional landmark for him, but it was not something he cared to undergo all that often. Or could afford to.

(He was still repaying the $7,000 for his client's funeral expenses during this time, having made an arrangement with Rajoo Casket to pay in installments. When he defaulted on one of the installments, a representative from

Rajoo actually came stomping into his office and began ranting and raving about the missed payment. Martin was finally able to placate this fellow, but the incident did little to calm his own already frazzled nerves during this difficult period.)

As he started to put the highly contentious case behind him, Martin reflected on what had really been accomplished. He had hoped to get the people of Singapore thinking about the critical issues in the case, to widen public awareness of how the judicial system here worked and also to get large numbers of Singaporeans asking if this was indeed a system that needed no reforms or refinements. The whole question of executions was of major importance to him, as was the question of who gets executed here and why.

Despite the apathy shown by his fellow citizens, he had believed that the various articles in the island's leading newspapers would have drawn more of a response, more empathy from those reading the accounts. Martin had clearly been heartened by that one Singaporean Indian woman who had read about the case and came to do something, no matter how small, to express her dismay at the possibility that someone might be hanged wrongly with all injustice attendant on that.

Remembering what this woman had said about her friends, Martin wondered how many other people had read those articles and been moved, had wanted to come and give support to Vignes' family, but decided against it. Perhaps there were a good many of them out there, thinking they should attend the wake, but family or friends had managed to talk them out of dropping by, if only for a short time and if only to express sympathy and concern.

Actually, there was at least one other person who read the reports of the three hearings and was quite impressed, stirred even. This particular individual would have loved to come and express his sympathy to all involved. He also would have liked to speak to Attorney Martin at some length on his work. But this person was unable to come. It was, in fact, simply not possible for him to get out.

As it happens, Martin did not tackle another drug case for almost a year and a half. And when it came his way, it was not just another drug case - it was another capital drug offence.

This case was significantly different from the Vignes Mourthi matter, however. (Nonetheless, the outcome was the same.) The defendant this time was not a Malaysian commuter-worker but a native Singaporean. In fact, this man had been something of a Singaporean hero up until a few years before his arrest. Moreover, this case did not involve heroin, only cannabis. And the defendant did not claim to be wholly innocent - he merely insisted that the charges against him were greatly overdrawn. He, too, sought simple justice, even if it meant a jail term on lesser charges.

The defendant in this affair was that same man who had read about Martin's battle in the cause of Vignes, and had wanted to come to the wake and funeral but was unable to. And the reason he was unable to come just at that time was that he himself happened to be in remand custody for drug dealing.

The defendant in this case was Shanmugam Murugesu, who was 36 years old when he was arrested on drug charges on 29 August 2003, roughly one month before the execution of Vignes. Crossing over from Malaysia, Shanmugam was stopped at the less heavily travelled Tuas Checkpoint. He had just pulled up to the checkpoint's Green Channel, indicating he had nothing to declare, when the border police there waved Shanmugam over to the side. There, they conducted what was probably a routine search on his motorcycle. During the search, they found packets of cannabis stuffed in the two carrier boxes mounted on either side of his cycle and under his driver's seat; six packets in all. These six packets were later determined to contain 1,029.8 grams of cannabis, and 880.89 grams of cannabis mixture: over double the legal limit for mere possession in Singapore.

With that amount of cannabis, Shanmugam was deemed by the authorities to be a dealer and charged accordingly. The accused did not argue with them. In fact, he admitted that he was a dealer - but a very small-time dealer. He was unaware, he adamantly maintained, that he was transporting anywhere near the amount of cannabis they found on his bike. Like Vignes Mourthi, Shanmugam swore that he was being used by his own supplier. Only this time, the detainee also admitted to a certain measure of his own guilt.

Shanmugam acknowledged having knowingly brought a single packet from Malaysia into Singapore, with the intention of passing it along to another dealer. All he was required to do, he testified, was to transport the cannabis into Singapore, then leave it at an arranged drop-off point. (This single packet was later determined to contain just 237 grams of cannabis, less than half the amount which carries the death penalty.) Shanmugam also admitted that he needed the $2,000 he hoped to earn from delivering the drugs to cover various pressing expenses. He swore, however, that the other five packets of weed must have been placed on his bike by his supplier back in Johor Bahru.

Shanmugam even sought to exonerate himself somewhat by throwing a net towards the bigger fish back in JB. He gave the Singapore authorities the name of an ethnic Chinese man whom he swore had supplied him with the drugs. To make things even easier for the police, Shanmugam provided them with this supplier's phone number in Malaysia. However, the authorities later said that when they called that number, the person on the other end claimed not to have ever heard of such a man. With that, they declared the trail cold. As far as the Singapore police were concerned, they had the man they wanted and needed to trawl no further.

Shanmugam (known to many of his friends simply as 'Sam') had first run into this supplier, whom he knew only as Mr Mok, when he was asked to repair the man's motorboat. This was several months before his arrest, evidently sometime in May 2003. As described by Sam, Mok was a Malaysian citizen of Chinese ancestry in his thirties with various business activities. After a short acquaintance, Mr Mok revealed that he also dabbled in the drug trade and that if Sam were interested, he could help him out with his financial problems. All this 'help' would involve was bringing small quantities of drugs like cannabis into Singapore and selling the stash.

At first, the former Singapore career soldier refused the offer of dealing, though he did occasionally purchase drugs for his own use. However, buried under continuing financial obligations that he had trouble meeting, Shanmugam eventually took up this man, Mok's proposal. However, he reportedly stipulated that he would only deal in cannabis, and then only in small amounts. Soon however, the odds caught up with him and landed him in a tight cell in Queenstown Remand Prison.

It was while he was in Queenstown that Sam read about the Vignes Mourthi case and R. Martin's determined efforts to secure a new trial for the young man. The cannabis dealer felt that Martin would be just the man to handle his own case and get the fairest outcome possible for him.

Until his world had started falling apart a few years earlier, Shanmugam could have served as a model Singaporean success story. Having grown up in poverty, the eldest child in a struggling Indian Singaporean family (he had a younger sister and brother), Shanmugam was determined to make something of himself. Backed by a loving, supportive mother, Shanmugam worked hard to grab his share of the Singapore dream and make his family proud of him. (His parents divorced in the late 90's, around the time their eldest son was starting to experience troubles of his own in his rather rocky marriage.)

Sam had been a fairly good student all throughout primary school. His favourite subjects were in the technical and practical areas. But when he entered secondary school, he fell in with some questionable companions and his grades started to suffer. Suffer badly, actually: he had to repeat Secondary 1, then failed Secondary 2 as well. At this point, his mother Letchumi, in many ways a quite traditional, conservative Tamil mother, decided the best course was to get her son out of this environment and into one offering more discipline and direction.

So as Shanmugam, now 14, was preparing to have one more go at Secondary 2, Letchumi used all the influence she could muster to get her son into Boys' School, something like the Singapore equivalent of military academy, where discipline was strongly stressed. This also entailed significant sacrifices on the family's part as they had to pay higher fees for this school. But it was worth it: Sam's marks improved significantly. Indeed, he excelled in motor and engine repair classes.

The Boys' School was a fast-track to the army, which is exactly where Shanmugam ended up four years later. He chalked up a solid record in his near decade in the active service, and continued to distinguish himself while in the army reserves. (All able-minded Singaporean men of sound mind are required to do reserve duty after their active duty, up through the age of 40.)

Following on his favourite subjects at school, Sam was especially fond of driving army vehicles, including tanks. Good with his hands and gifted with an agile mind, he soon became quite adept at the maintenance and repair of various vehicles. Something of a model soldier, he eventually made his way up to the rank of sergeant. He seemed destined for the officers' ranks and a long career in the military.

However, his marriage at the age of 21 signalled a brake to his advancement in the army. Before long, he found himself the father of twin sons. The demands on his time the military made were not the best thing for a man with a family of four. Not long after the birth of his sons, Sam decided to switch his energies to the civilian sector. He left the armed forces voluntarily.

Sam had served eight years in the Singapore Army as a combat engineer, before moving on to another, even more admired field: that of sports star.

Even though he would later, in deep depression, stop competing, sports had long played an important role in Shanmugam Murugesu's life and he always remained proud of his athletic accomplishments, both individual and for his country. And the sport at which he most distinguished himself was the exciting water sport of jet skiing.

Jet skiing, which began in the U.S. in the 1970's, is not a sport for sissies. In fact, it is frequently classified as an extreme sport, and a British website recently voiced fears that it could soon disappear in the UK simply because insurance rates for participants had sky-rocketed. This sport entails participants racing along the waters at great speeds in small personal watercraft.

As an early report on the sport, published in the San Diego Union, portrayed it, those daring sports enthusiasts perched on Jet Ski watercraft were "...skimming the water behind a pair of motorcycle-type handlebars testing a new type of water scooter." The article went on to describe how the "stand-up scooters" appeared to offer their riders the "...thrills of water skiing without the need of a towboat." The thrills are indeed many in this sport, but thrills are usually aligned to risks; jet skiing is loaded with risks.

It was a challenging activity that appealed to something deep within Shanmugam, who loved a good challenge. He took up the sport with gusto after his release from the army and soon became one of the top jet ski competitors in the Island Republic. He even represented Singapore in major events such as the 1995 World Championship Jet Ski Finals in Lake Havasu, Arizona, USA, bringing home a medal from this competition, thus giving a huge boost to Singapore's international image as a sports nation.

But jet skiing was not the only sport Shanmugam actively participated in. He was also involved in motorbike racing, deep-sea diving, boating and rope-climbing: all of them, sports that entail significant risks. It was obvious that Shanmugam was a risk-taker, a distinguishing quality in a society short of risk-takers. This was one reason why he stood out.

But unlike all too many male athletes, Shanmugam Murugesu was not a standard macho type. In fact, he was known here as a 'girl's guy', meaning that he was unusually sensitive and could always lend a sympathetic ear to women who wanted to talk about their problems and get a male perspective on them. Shanmugam had a lot of female friends; just friends, that is, with no romantic attachments. This, too, is unusual for male athletes here in Southeast Asia. (Not typical for male athletes anywhere, come to think of it.)

As a result of his athletic achievements, Shanmugam Murugesu was named to the prestigious Singapore Sports Council, where he served for two terms, a total of 4 years.

But he didn't only race the jet ski boats, he also became adept at the maintenance and repair of these vehicles. His keen interests in tending to motorised vehicles from his army days carried over quite smoothly into civilian life. As Sam's involvement in water sports grew, he soon became quite accomplished at repairing various types of boats. He started doing it for friends and acquaintances, then for friends of friends. For all these reasons, Shanmugam Murugesu had become a very popular man in the area. On the surface, just about everything seemed to be going his way.

But just under that surface, there were serious problems brewing, mainly with his wife. This union had actually been an arranged marriage, to a first cousin on his mother's side from India. It never quite morphed into a storybook version of wedded bliss.

The tensions between the two continued growing and when Shanmugam came home one evening unexpectedly to find his wife entertaining a boyfriend, he took his two boys and left the home he had shared with his wife. He moved in temporarily with his mother "for the sake of his sons": he did not want them growing up in an environment where marital infidelity was blatantly practiced.

It wasn't long before Shanmugam's wife turned her back fully on the others and effectively abandoned the family, leaving Sam to care for their two sons. In the meantime, she had moved in with a boyfriend, making any attempt at reconciliation virtually impossible. The couple were divorced in 2001, with Shanmugam being awarded custody of his twin sons, then 12-years old.

In the aftermath of the break-up of his marriage and subsequent divorce, the former golden boy found himself in an emotional tailspin. He lost interest in many of the activities which had enriched his life before that. This once-passionate sportsman had even largely given up sports.

But it wasn't just depression over the failure of his marriage that caused

Shanmugam to give up these activities. Now a single-parent, he had to look after his two young sons, along with his mother and his sister. (Following a spinal operation five years earlier, Madam Letchumi was unable to work and became completely dependent on her two sons for support.) He didn't really have the time, let alone the wherewithal, to continue with some of his other former free-time activities.

Things started to pick up again for Shanmugam shortly after his separation from his wife when he met Lynn (Taff), an attractive American woman working here in Singapore as a kindergarten teacher. The two fell in love and became very close quite quickly. They took a trip to India together, wherein the magic of that enchanting country enriched their relationship. Lynn also got along well with Sam's twin sons. The couple made plans to marry, plans which included a relocation to India where they would open up a hotel together. After his arranged marriage, flawed from the start, Shanmugam seemed to have found the woman he needed to make everything complete.

But it wasn't to be. Lynn started to have doubts about permanently settling in such a different world (India) and also wondered if she would be able to handle suddenly having two teenage sons, with all the responsibilities that entailed. With no small amount of pain, she decided to back out and returned to America. This loss was even more overwhelming for Sam than the collapse of his marriage had been. He needed to begin all over again - for a second time.

Unfortunately, he had taken up one new activity in the interim: drugs. He had turned to illicit drugs in the aftermath of his break-up with Lynn. As far as anyone close to him knows, Shanmugam restricted his drug use to cannabis. Like millions of users around the world, he found that ganja (the Malay word for cannabis) helped to relax him in moments of stress. And this was a period of enormous stress for him.

Further, he was apparently only an occasional user of the drug and then usually in social situations. When with a group of friends or colleagues, if someone said they knew where they could lay their hands on some weed, Shanmugam would generally join in. This, however, typically entailed everyone in the group throwing in 20 or 30 Singapore dollars to make the purchase. This, of course, did not make his tight financial situation any healthier.

Drugs had in no way taken over his life, however. He managed to maintain two physically demanding jobs along with occasional pick-up jobs repairing boats. More importantly, he served as a good father to his sons. He knew how important it was that they have a strong, responsible parent as a role model - especially in the absence of their mother. (All this suggests that Sam indeed only abused marijuana, a mild drug with few lingering effects.) Just prior to his arrest, Shanmugam had been working as a taxi-driver and a free-lance window cleaner to support his sons and himself.

He had also started to pick up odd jobs repairing boats at a repair shed in Johor Bahru, Malaysia. (The border town where Vignes Mourthi had lived up till his arrest.) An acquaintance whom he knew only as Ah Seng would call him to say there was a boat in need of repairs. Could Sam come up and work on it - for a decent fee, of course. Shanmugam naturally leapt at this opportunity and was soon nicely supplementing his main income with this repair work.

The work was almost always carried out at a go-kart track at the edge of JB. The track boasted excellent facilities for such work, with well-equipped repair sheds and a group of like-minded motor enthusiasts. Sam, by and large a very affable fellow who made friends easily, soon had a number of part-time buddies there, as well as eager customers.

One of the clients Ah Seng linked Sam up with was this shadowy figure, Mr Mok. It would prove to be a darkly fateful meeting. Mok had a motorboat, the boat had some problems, and Sam was just the man to fix them. Mok and Shanmugam become somewhat friendly. As Shanmugam later recalled it, the two men hit it off on their very first meeting and at the end of their discussion on boat repairs, they sealed their new professional relationship by smoking some cannabis together, with a few other friends from the repair sheds joining in.

Many of those who knew him well recall that Sam, despite the many personal problems he had suffered, remained a very trusting person; indeed, often trusting to the point of gullible. It was this gullibility that may have proven his undoing done when he put too much trust in this man Mok. Despite the easy friendship the two had forged, loud alarms should have sounded in Sam's head when his 'friend' Mok started leading him into rather murky legal waters .

Meanwhile, this divorced single father was providing not just for his two sons but also for his mother and, in addition, helping out his sister Mahes, by then herself a single parent with two young children. (Mahes had separated from her husband in 1997 or 1998, shortly before Sam parted ways with his wife. She is still waiting for her divorce to be finalised.) His mother, 62 years old at the time of the ordeal, was in frail health and living in virtual poverty. But it wasn't only family members that Sam showed generosity towards: it was later pointed out that as a taxi-driver, he would often allow the severely handicapped to ride free in his cab, even though it took away from the earnings he could have used for his family and himself. He also showed a generosity to friends that one would not have expected from someone in his financially tight situation.

Ironically, Sam's younger brother Kuben was a police officer and had even been seconded for a short time to Singapore's Central Narcotics Bureau. (Though he was a member of Singapore's Marine Police at the time of Shanmugam's arrest.) This former army professional and Sports Council member would certainly have been aware of Singapore's harsh drug laws. Moreover, except for one minor traffic offence, Shanmugam did not have any previous convictions before that unlucky day in August 2003.

The SSC-scape

The Singapore Sports Council (SSC) is a statutory board of the Government of Singapore, established by an Act of Parliament under the SSC Act of 1973. Headquartered at Singapore's National Stadium, it falls under the supervision of the Ministry of Community Development, Youth and Sports. The SSC operates a wide range of sports facilities all across Singapore. Its main role is to promote sports participation for all Singaporeans.

The SSC is comprised of a Chairman, a Deputy Chairman and 5 to 12 members from the public and private sectors. They are appointed by the Minister of Sports for a term of two years. Most of those who sit on the Council are CEOs and managing directors of leading companies in the Republic, parliamentary secretaries, and high-ranking military officers. The fact that Shanmugam was appointed to the Council twice was quite an honour, especially for a boy who had grown up in poverty and had to repeat two years in secondary school.

Shanmugam's earnings as a taxi-driver and window-washer were rather meagre, and month after month, he found it increasingly hard to make ends meet - especially as he was looking after others. At times, as he later said, he would sit and ponder his financial problems, then break down in tears when he thought of how his family might suffer if things got any worse. Finally, he decided to take an easy route out of his financial problems and deal in illicit drugs to get him over the hump. He had been doing this for about four months when he was pulled over that day at the Tuas checkpoint.

When he was caught, Sam clearly knew the drill: he readily admitted to the crime, though he argued that he believed he was only carrying one packet, with contents of what he took to be between 200 and 300 grams. As he repeatedly explained, knowing the fatal consequences of being caught with over 500 grams of the drug, he did not dare to take that risk. Especially considering the number of other people who so depended on him. He cooperated with the authorities, within days flipping the bigger fish who had supplied him with the cannabis to the CNB officers.

Sam even sought to cut a deal with the Public Prosecutor's office: he would forego a trial, with all its costs, and confess in open court to possession of 499 grams of cannabis. This is one gram under the amount that carries an automatic death penalty upon conviction.

It's also a judicial convenience that the Public Prosecutor's office often serves up when they decide to make a deal. They know many accused dealers will seize the offer and serve a prison term, pay a fine, even perhaps get caned, but escape the possibility of the noose. Which is why you'll see that so many high-profile cases involving cannabis in Singapore happen to involve exactly 499 grams. (Or even more dramatically, 499.9 grams.)

But for whatever reasons, the Prosecutor's office turned down Shanmugam's offer and opted for the full trial on the most serious charges. Shanmugam Murugesu suddenly found himself facing a fight for his life. And he knew the odds were most definitely not in his favour.

All too aware of his family's parlous financial situation, Shanmugam elected to go with a court-appointed attorney for his criminal trial. He did not see this as too great a risk. In his view, he had a good case for escaping the noose. He even believed that they could still strike a deal in the courtroom, getting the charges reduced to mere possession. With all this in mind, Shanmugam turned over his fate to his court-appointed counsel, a Mr Ganesan, assisted by Rajah Retnam, who had also been assigned to the case by the court.

Before and after, in particular at his trial, Shanmugam ardently maintained that he had only knowingly brought in that single packet, containing under 300 grams. He had insisted on keeping the stash comfortably until the 500 grams level as he knew that any possession of 500 grams or above carried an automatic death sentence. He may have been a little too trusting of some people, but he was certainly not stupid.

In contrast to the friction-packed Vignes Mourthi-Moorthy Angappan trial, which dragged on for many months and saw a parade of witnesses and rebuttals, Shanmugam Murugesu's drug trial ran a mere four days. The only witnesses called were the defendant himself, arresting and interrogating officers, police recorders and the police department's Tamil-language interpreter. There was something of an imbalance in the testimonies, actually: the prosecution called 23 witnesses while Shanmugam himself was the sole witness on the defence side.

This huge imbalance in testimonies reflects the single track of the argumentation. This case was nowhere near as complicated or convoluted as the

Vignes Mourthi case had been. Both sides agreed that the defendant was knowingly transporting an illegal drug into Singapore and was caught in the act. There was also no debate as to whether or not six packets of cannabis had been recovered from various compartments on Shanmugam's bike. The only point of dispute was how much of that drug the defendant had knowingly brought in. And, of course, the difference in the answers provided was literally a difference of life and death for Shanmugam.

The trial opened on 19 April 2004 and closed on the 23rd. The prosecution's case filled the first two days, the defence made its case on the third day, while the fourth day was given over to the two sides making their submissions. On that same day, the judge issued his verdict.

The entire case turned on whether the additional five packets of cannabis, bringing the total to over 1 kilogram, had been planted on his bike or not. From the first of September 2003, Shanmugam continued to insist that it had been. He was not sure who had planted it, he admitted, but his main suspect was his acquaintance Mok, the Chinese Malaysian who had supplied him with the first bag of cannabis.

There were two major facts standing against Shanmugam. When arrested, he waited three days before mentioning the shadowy Mok and their agreement that Sam would only smuggle in one small bag of cannabis containing less than 500 grams. Further, during the long hours of his interrogation, the accused had signed a confession saying that he had brought in all six packets, as found in the two main carrier bags and under his seat. (Earlier in the interrogation marathon and at the trial, Sam said the additional packets were probably slipped into these hiding places on the bike while he was engaged repairing a boat.)

Further, Shanmugam himself believed that someone had put the finger on him, informing customs agents to stop the man on this particular bike. There was a tip-off, he thought, and that's why the police net was thrown over him. The most likely candidate, again, was Mok. The reason he had at first kept quiet about Mok was that he didn't wish to drag this fellow whom he had liked and trusted into the matter until it dawned on him that Mok himself was probably the cause of all this trouble. Also, he didn't want to mention the cannabis activities at the go-kart track because many of his buddies and associates there would, from time to time, share some ganja and he had no wish to bring any heat down upon them. Unfortunately, the trial judge did not accept this show of loyalty; he eventually decided that the three-day delay in coming up with the identity of Mok rendered the account "highly unlikely to be true".

His explanation for the signed statements was what he described as severe intimidation during his interrogation, with officers shouting at him and even slapping him on the side of his head several times. (In Singapore, suspects have no right to legal counsel during interrogations and very rarely do any lawyers even get to see their clients during the early stages of their confinement. Charges of unfair intimidation are rampant, including those made by police officers against other police personnel. *See Aftermaths.*

The prosecution denied that there had been any such intimidation. They also argued that the only reason the defendant had come up with the theory of someone surreptitiously stashing an extra five packets onto his motorcycle was to cover his own intentions to deliver or sell a larger amount of cannabis and earn the appropriately higher sales. The prosecution gave no ground whatsoever in arguing for conviction on the most serious charges, with the ultimate penalty linked to such a conviction.

As mentioned, the judge did not have to mull over the testimonies and arguments of the two sides very long. On the last day, the prosecution wrapped up its submission shortly before twelve. Judge Tay Yong Kwang adjourned to his chambers at 11:46 a.m. to go through all the arguments. Court reconvened at 11:59am. The defendant was asked to rise; a sombre judge informed him that he was "satisfied beyond a reasonable doubt that the prosecution has proved the charges against you and I therefore find you guilty as charged - and I convict you accordingly." He then passed a sentence of death upon the convicted man. The Deputy Public Prosecutor then withdrew the two remaining lesser charges against Shanmugam (one of these dropped charges was for the possession of 880.89 grams of cannabis mixture), with the remaining minor legal matters being tidied up quickly.

Chapter 12

MOVING FOR JUSTICE

The truth is violated by falsehood, but outraged by silence.

- Old adage

The case then entered the appeals stage, an automatic process when a death sentence is passed in Singapore. Shanmugam Murugesu had one more chance - but only this one - to try to prove himself innocent of the more serious charges and so escape the noose. He had to make the best of it. Realising the difficulties he faced, he decided he could not rely on a court-appointed attorney this time around. He would have to stretch the financial resources of his family well past the breaking point and engage a first-rate lawyer to defend him before the appeals panel.

Sam's second attorney was Peter Fernando, who had handled many drug cases throughout his career. He boasts an enviable record of successful defences. However, this kind of cachet and expertise does not come without a price; the family had to pay this high-octane lawyer $15,000 to handle Shanmugam's appeal. Fernando was assisted in this appeal by Amarick Gill.

The defendant's appeal was filed on 25 October 2004. It read something like the appeal made earlier on behalf of Vignes Mourthi: the original verdict should be overturned as the trial judge had simply given too much weight to the prosecution's claims in making his verdict. The reasonable doubts regarding the defendant's guilt should have tipped the balance in his favour, with the judge convicting him on the lesser charge, sending him off to prison but sparing him from the gallows.

The appeal was heard before the three-judge Appeals tribunal on 14 January of the following year. Again, the tribunal was headed by Singapore's Chief Justice Yong Pung How, joined on this coram by Chow Hick Tin and Kan Ting Chiu. Fernando more or less repeated the arguments he had made in his written appeal. The prosecution, represented by DPP Seah Kim Ming Glenn, basically repeated the case they had presented during the original trial. The appeal was, predictably, dismissed. Now, like so many others on Singapore's death row, the prisoner could only sit and hope for a presidential clemency.

And this is where Attorney R. Martin once again entered the fray, after the official appeal had failed. This time, however, the zealous lawyer took up the cause before the President's clemency ruling was issued, already recognising the odds against getting a clemency ruling. (Remember, only six of those have been issued in Singapore's 40 years as a republic).

Still beset with the painful memories of the Vignes Mourthi ordeal and how all his diligent efforts had failed to save that young man's life, Martin decided that he and Shanmugam's family had to pursue this battle armed with a dynamic new strategy. This time, it wouldn't be enough to wage the battle just in the established courts; this time, they would open up a second front and take the contentious matter into the court of public opinion.

Martin quickly developed a close relationship with the whole family during this period. (He had again taken the case on a pro bono basis, as he was well aware the family did not have the resources to pay his usual fee.) After talking to Sam's brother Kuben, Martin made his way to Changi Prison to speak with the prisoner himself.

Unlike the Vignes Mourthi case, where Martin never once visited his client in prison, Martin had a number of face-to-face encounters with Shanmugam at the Changi facility. These meetings all took place in the prison's Interview Room, where attorney and client are separated by thick glass and conversations are facilitated by small, unseen microphones.

Their first meeting was quite upbeat: Sam was thrilled to come face-to-face with the attorney whose work had once inspired him. In fact, he even pulled out a copy of one of the Straits Times articles that had appeared during the previous death penalty ordeal to show the lawyer. Martin was quite touched to see that this man, with all his own pressing concerns, had kept that particular article for close to a year and a half.

For the most part, Sam kept smiling and in fairly good spirits during this first encounter. He, too, was well aware that the odds were strongly against him at this stage, but he felt slightly buoyed just to know that there was more attention being given to his cause and that dedicated hope was coming.

Martin left this meeting in a more upbeat spirit himself. Shanmugam Murugesu was a handsome, rather charismatic man readily given to flashing that huge, boyish smile that endeared him to male and female friends alike.

Not long after this meeting with the condemned man, Martin met Sam's mother, Letchumi Ammah, at her home in the Jurong section of the island. Sam's background was similar to Martin's: a working-class family, the same language (working-class Tamil) used in the home. In her Indian sarong, Letchumi actually reminded Martin of his own mother. As he recalls it, this first encounter was "as if my mother was there, pleading for help". Shortly after having met Letchumi, the lawyer also met Sam's twin sons at the same Jurong West HDB flat. Just 14, they were rather shy and not terribly outgoing - just the opposite of their father. Still, they were very keen about Martin's coming on board and asked him what they themselves could do to try to save their father from the noose. Their diffidence would not keep them from playing a significant role in the campaign.

Not surprisingly for a somewhat traditional, conservative Tamil mother, Letchumi Ammah was devastated when she first heard that her son had been arrested for dealing in drugs: drugs, of all things. At first, the family had even tried to keep the true story away from Sam's two sons. They were told that he had gone overseas for a time. But when they both kept on trying to contact their father by phone or some other way, the boys were told the disturbing truth. It was not easy to take for 12-year-old boys living in strait-laced Singapore.

In the petition to the President for clemency, which Sam's appeal lawyers had prepared, the team cited six cases from just the previous two years in which individuals had been arrested for possession of cannabis wherein the amount was officially reduced to 499 grams or even 499.9 grams, allowing the defendants to escape the noose. In five of the cited cases, the original amounts of cannabis had been higher than what Shanmugam himself was caught transporting. The plea also mentioned that Sam had been ready to cut such a deal with the prosecuting attorneys but found his offer spurned, with no reason given.

The petition also included letters attesting to his character from his two sons, both of his parents, his former girlfriend, now living back in America and from his brother Kuben, the Singapore policeman. The case for clemency looked good, but Martin felt it needed something more. And there wasn't much time before the President made a decision.

Martin quickly came up with what he thought might be an effective PR campaign: printing up hundreds of flyers on the case and distributing them. These flyers were handed out primarily at Centrepoint, a popular shopping and dining complex along Singapore's busy Orchard Road. While Sam's two sons played the major role in the distribution, other volunteers also came forward to help out. The local press took notice of this unusual action and gave the story some valuable space. Photos of the twins offering flyers to

Your Silence Is Requested

In turning down the application for Amnesty's Tim Parritt to speak at the Death Penalty Forum, Singapore's Ministry of Foreign Affairs issued the following statement on 16 April 2005: "The Minister for Home Affairs has rejected the Open Singapore Centre's appeal of 15 April 2005 for a Professional Visit Pass for a Mr Tim Parritt to speak at its public forum."

"Singapore has a well-respected and independent judiciary. Its legal and judicial system has been consistently rated highly in international and regional rankings for its integrity and transparency. Our legal system was rated top just last year in a Political and Economic Risk Consultancy (Perc) survey on the quality and integrity of its judicial system, for the

fourth year running." "Singapore has one of the most fair and transparent legal systems in the world. We do not require a foreigner to tell Singapore and Singaporeans how our criminal justice system should function."

Nevertheless, as he sat mum up on the stage with the other invited guests at the forum, Mr Parritt's enforced silence proved quite eloquent.

passers-by made for good attention-grabbers in the papers.

From this action, the initially small group began to attract the attention and support of many, including some opposition political figures, such as Dr. Chee Soon Juan, the head of the Singapore Democratic Party and a long-time campaigner for civil rights. After discussing a number of key issues around this particular case, Attorney Martin and Dr. Chee decided to organise a forum on the death penalty itself, with a focus on the impending execution of Shanmugam. New flyers announcing this forum and inviting all those interested to attend were handed out at Centrepoint in the week before the conclave.

The forum was held at the Asia Hotel near the popular Newton Circus hawkers' centre, on 16 April, a Saturday afternoon. The response from the general public was encouraging, to say the least. Organisers had anticipated a crowd of some 70 people, but over double that number turned out. Extra chairs had to be brought in, but even so, many people ended up standing, packed in the side aisles and along the back of the room. Some of those packed in even started to feel faint, and had to be escorted out to the corridors for some air. Also present were Sam's mother and two sons, who sat quietly off to the side of the stage during most of the event.

Talks on the death penalty issue were given by a number of prominent local figures, including the condemned man's lawyer. Co-organiser Dr. Chee also gave a lively talk, complete with projections and power point.

The emotional highpoint of this forum was a plea by Letchumi Ammah for her son's life. This brief appeal, delivered in Tamil, then translated into English by R. Martin, came at the tail end of the full-bodied speeches and stirred almost everyone in the room with the sincerity and force of its feeling. It even brought tears to the eyes of some of the listeners.

Tim Parritt from Amnesty International (London) had been invited to speak at this forum, and he flew in from Kuala Lumpur specifically for the event. However, one day before the actual event, the Singapore government informed Parritt that he had been denied permission to speak at any public gathering, including the Asia Hotel forum. He was still free to come in and visit Singapore, but he couldn't open his mouth before any public gathering while there. If he did speak, he could very well be arrested.

But Parritt still wished to show his solidarity with the cause, so he came to the forum, took his assigned place of honour, then sat silent on the stage with the other scheduled speakers while his prepared speech was read out by the event's moderator, Madame Salbiah Ahmad.

The forum's moderator, Salbiah Ahmad, herself drew some unsolicited attention from the authorities later. As the forum was winding down, she had just asked if there were any further questions from the floor. (Those in attendance had raised a number of important questions earlier.) Suddenly, the moderator was approached onstage by a pair of plainclothes police officers. They asked this respected civil rights activist and trained lawyer, who is an ethnic Malay, if she was a Singaporean citizen. When she replied that she indeed was, they asked to see her IC, or national identity card, which she promptly produced for them.

Although the police officers issued no instructions about wrapping up the meeting right then and there, the interruption proved an effective, even dramatic, way of bringing down the curtain on the event. No further questions were asked, and despite the fact that there was still a good deal of energy in the crowd, the forum was duly brought to a close.

But the forum's impact produced a number of interesting ripples. A flock of people from the local arts community attended this conclave and immediately took deep interest in the cause of the condemned cannabis dealer. They decided that they could contribute their small part to the cause by putting together a three-hour-plus vigil with music, poetry, perhaps even dance and theatre to energise the arts producers and consumers in Singapore on this matter.

There was also an encouraging representation of the local and international press at the event, giving the cause the kind of growing coverage the organisers had hoped for. Amongst the publications and wire services that had sent reporters were the AP, the AFP and Reuters. (The local press was represented by major newspapers such as Today and the Straits Times.)

The atmosphere at the forum was highly charged, almost from the beginning, and the energy kept building as the event moved along. By the time the meeting broke up - or was broken up - around 5:30 p.m., the enthusiasm was still bubbling, so the organisers, led by Martin and Dr. Chee (who had also spoken at the forum) decided to channel this energy into positive action. A dedicated group of about 30 people headed off to the Istana to make yet another personal appeal to the president to grant clemency. They arrived at the Istana around six o'clock, bent on making this appeal as effective as possible. In at least one regard, it produced undeniable effects: observers noted there were probably more police than petitioners there, many of them ISD (Internal Security Department) officers.

As a seasoned attorney, Martin was well aware of the prevailing law on petitioning in the Republic, so he told the 30-strong contingent that they needed to break up into groups of four or less to petition for clemency; without an official licence to assemble, groups of five or more are considered 'illegal gatherings' under Singapore law. Hence, the gates around the Istana were ringed with tight groups of four or fewer petitioners. There was, it should be noted, no police interference with any of the groups or individual petitioners.

The most dramatic moment in this impromptu demonstration came when Shanmugam's mother and both sons knelt down before the Istana's gates and implored the president to grant the convicted man a reprieve from his death sentence.

A Reuters photographer had gone with the group to shoot photos of these spontaneous protests. Over the next few days, photos appeared in publications around the globe showing the mother and two boys kneeling before the Istana. The impact was startling. Never before in the history of the city-state had an impending presidential clemency ruling drawn such widespread attention.

Less than a week after this highly encouraging forum, President Nathan did issue his ruling; sadly, despite all the activities of the previous few weeks, the appeal was rejected. Shanmugam was now facing the noose sometime in the very near future - perhaps even just one week later.

As per protocol, the President's decision was sent directly to the prisoner's lawyer. The missive was short and very much to the point: clemency had been denied. Even though he had "quasi-expected" such a ruling, Martin experienced a sickly feeling as he read it. He shook his head; he couldn't understand this president, denying clemency to a man who seemed to be a perfect candidate for such a salutary show of mercy. What had gone through the Head of State's head as he weighed all the factors in coming to this decision?

It was now Martin's unenviable task to inform the family. He travelled out to their home in the Jurong West section of the island with an associate, to lend him moral support in this sad duty. Only Letchumi, the condemned man's mother, and her elderly aunt were at home when he got there.

When he told them the bad news, Shanmugam's mother stared blankly into space, as if this message was somehow scraped against the tight air of the room, in some hard-to-decipher code. For a few minutes, she just stood there, numb with shock. Then, as the shock wore off, Letchumi first started beating her own face with her fists, then dropped her hands and started drumming hard on her chest. Finally, she screamed and almost collapsed on the floor in grief. Well aware of her poor physical health, Martin was afraid she was about to have a stroke, or maybe already in the throes of one.

Martin and his associate rushed over to the woman, to see that she was not having a stroke or some kind of seizure. They then started to help her up. Letchumi's aunt, herself rather old and quite frail, joined them and offered whatever assistance she could to get her distraught niece back on her feet. Though Letchumi is a small woman with a slight frame, the task was not quite as easy as it looked; the tensions and pain in her body seemed to have taken on an intense weight of their own.

The clemency letter from President Nathan was dated 22 April, though it only arrived at Martin's office, via snail mail, on 26 April. Martin, who had never before been the recipient of such a notification was surprised at the rather cold handling of this matter; he had assumed that such a missive would have been delivered by hand on the day of its issue. He thought that the head of state, generally known for his courtesy and congeniality, could have accorded this one small courtesy to the family of a condemned man.

Ironically enough, Shanmugam had received a medal for his achievements as an army reservist, which was presented to him around the time of the clemency decision. Obviously, the clemency committee had not allowed this honour, or any of the previous honours, to influence them in their deliberations.

But there were still two major events lined up before the scheduled execution. One was that vigil with entertainment being organised by prominent members of the local arts community along with the ThinkCentre, a local organisation which serves as an advocate for a wide range of human rights issues. The lead organisers on this event were Lee Weng Choy of The Substation Arts Complex and Lucy Davis, along with Samydorai Sinnappan, head of the ThinkCentre.

The original plan was to hold the event at The Substation, centrally located and familiar to many people in Singapore. In addition to these two prime advantages, The Substation offered a large garden performance area at the rear of the complex that would have been ideal for such an event. The various acts could perform in the open air with a large open stage; moreover, a candlelight vigil for the condemned prisoner could be held there with no fear of violating fire laws or endangering participants.

However, as the organisers were putting the final touches on their plans, they were informed by the police that they would almost certainly be denied a licence for such an event held at The Substation. (As it was an open-air gathering, the authorities could, for instance, claim concerns that things would get out of control. In general, performance licences in Singapore are harder to secure for outdoor events.) Realising that the vigil itself, not the venue, was the essential thing, the organisers (now including Martin himself) decided to take the path of least official resistance and recast the vigil as a private affair in a hotel.

The group first approached the Golden Landmark Hotel on Beach Road and booked a reception room appropriate to their needs. The Think Centre had stepped forward as the official organiser and Samydorai Sinnappan, its head, managed to book the room. However, just three or four days before the scheduled event, the people at the Think Centre received a call from the Golden Landmark with some bad news: due to a sudden leaking roof in that room, they would have to cancel the event. Their advance reservation fee was returned.

Although there is no proof of this, many people involved with the vigil started mumbling that the booking was cancelled not due to any leak in the roof, but because of a leak to government security agencies. The speculation (and that's all it remains) was that these agencies, having gotten wind of the rally, put pressure on the hotel management to cancel the reservation and to use any convenient excuse to do so. Usually, the Singapore government does not have to put too much pressure on organisations or business establishments to get them to bend the government's way.

With the date for the event now just days away, the disappointed organisers quickly sought out another venue and found success with the Furama Hotel at the edge of Chinatown, not far from Martin's office. They managed to book a small reception hall there. This time, having twice been burnt, the organisers didn't volunteer too many specific details as to what the purpose of the planned gathering was; subsequently, there were no cancellations and the vigil finally went ahead more or less as planned.

Despite the double switching of the venues, and the fact that it was held on a Friday night when a number of other popular events were being held, a large number of people turned up at the vigil. What had started in small flickers during the Vignes Mourthi ordeal had begun to flare with this case: Singaporeans and Singapore residents from many walks of life became interested and involved in Shanmugam's plight. People were asking questions, reviewing the case, taking part in the forum and the vigil.

This was actually a broad coalition of people with varying agendas. A good many of those involved were strongly principled death-penalty opponents who saw Sam's case as a potent rallying point for their position. Some came on board because they felt that the condemned man in question might not have been accorded full justice in his trial or sentencing.

Others were not so much concerned with the issues of innocence and guilt surrounding the case: they simply felt that Shanmugam deserved clemency as he was now a single parent of two young boys and the main support of his ailing mother. More, his spotless record before this arrest as well as his contributions to the nation in the realms of national defence and sports earned him special consideration, these people reasoned.

Still others focused on the Shanmugam case because of their revulsion that a man should be executed simply for selling cannabis. As one local writer who attended the forum and vigil put it, "If they're going to execute this man for selling just over a kilo of cannabis, then they should also hang the top executives of British American Tobacco and Phillip Morris Singapore; those guys sell mega-tonnes of a product that's even more harmful than cannabis, but instead of getting strung up, they get fêted and honoured."

The vigil was held in the Canton Meeting Room of the hotel and ran for close to three hours. There were bands, solo musicians, an a cappella singer, and people reciting poetry or reading from relevant texts. There were also short talks on the issue at hand: R. Martin got up and spoke about the specifics of the Shanmugam case. Samydorai Sinnappan of the ThinkCentre delivered a heartfelt diatribe on the philosophical and moral dimensions of the death penalty. One woman, a local designer, even unveiled a special anti-death penalty T-shirt she had come up with for this campaign.

But not everyone who wanted to speak or read was allowed to. The reason: in addition to all those concerned about the pending execution and issues relating to this, a number of plainclothes police agents had dropped by. The vigil had been granted a permit for a public performance as there was music and singing involved. Had there only been speeches, there would have been no need of a permit as the meeting was held indoors. (Speeches held outdoors do require a special permit in Singapore.)

As a license had been applied for and granted, only those individuals who had been listed on the application as performers and speakers were allowed to address the assembly. Consequently, no unauthorised (i.e., those not listed) speakers were allowed to speak. An Open Mike session, where all those who wanted to express their feelings on the issue were invited to come forward and do so, was promptly truncated by the police. The first unlisted speaker to mount the stage and take the microphone happened to be V.A. Sivakumar of the Vallalar organisation, a Hindu group opposed to all killing for any reason. Sivakumar was stopped within the first minute of his talk. The plainclothes officers abruptly ended his talk, then took down his particulars.

The word about the gag order then spread throughout the gathering. All those who had been prepared to get up and express opinions, concerns or solidarity with the family and close friends of Shanmugam would have to confine their expressions to one-on-one exchanges. The Open Mike had been closed.

Sam's family members were also present at the vigil, sitting behind the main gathering. Sam's two sons tried looking brave, though the increasing strain of the ordeal was clear in their faces. The condemned man's mother also tried to look as brave as she could, though from time to time her suffering could not be contained and she would break out into wailing that served as a distressing undertone to the songs and speeches on the stage.

The mood at the end of the vigil was a strange mix of tossed emotions. On the one hand, some of the participants came away with warm feelings brought on by a shared sense of purpose in fighting a cause so long ignored in the Lion City as well as the encouraging music, singing and speeches in the name of this cause. On the other hand, most of those present were all too aware that all their efforts, all their talents, all their good wishes would probably have little or no effect in preventing the execution of the man they had come there to stand up for. The unambiguous pain on the faces of the family members, along with the mother's occasional wailing added to the uncomfortable feelings that many left with.

One special feature of this vigil was that those in attendance were invited to write short letters for Shanmugam. Lined sheets of paper were put out on a table at the rear of the hall. All these letters would be collected and handed to the condemned man in Changi Prison within a day or two.

The various letters offered sympathy, support, and outrage at what was soon to happen to this man. The letter-writers spanned a broad age spectrum, from young children to senior citizens. One of the notes that touched Shanmugam most was apparently written by a young child, perhaps only seven or eight years old. The condemned man appreciated that even someone this young could be taken up with his cause.

An article on this vigil appeared in Britain's respected Guardian the next day. Headed 'Singapore Finally Finds A Voice in Death Row Protest', the article proclaimed that history had been made there at the Furama Hotel, where "an unprecedented event for the tightly controlled island republic" had been held.

In addition, a reporter from the Guardian-Observer, John Aglionby, was sent from Jakarta to cover this groundbreaking event. The headline on

Aglionby's article, which appeared in that Sunday's Observer : "A Silence Broken". And there was, indeed, an invigorating sense of silence being broken.

Sadly, whatever this vigil did accomplish, it did not increase Shanmugam Murugesu's chances of escaping the noose at all. The execution date was set right after the vigil took place: Friday the 13th of May. Barring some miracle, the former Singapore sports hero had less than a week left.

That week, from Monday to Thursday, visiting hours for the condemned man were increased. Family members were allowed to see him from around 9 a.m. to 5 p.m. each of those days. There was, indeed, at least one member of the family with him during the entire allowed time all four of those days.

About a week before the execution date, the defence lawyer confided to his associate Violet Netto, that he felt the cause was beyond hope, that the chances of reversing the President's decision were somewhere between zero and null. Even so, he was determined to fight on, to do everything he could in the hope of some miracle happening. He owed that much to the family, he averred.

R. Martin was extremely exhausted for almost the entire first two weeks of May 2005. The campaign up to that point had left him close to exhaustion, especially as he had continued to represent and work for his other clients during this period. He found himself putting in something like 16 to 17-hour days during the final fortnight. The intensity of his work actually increased once the petition for clemency was turned down. As Martin recalls, "I had to crack my head as to how I could proceed through the legal system because there's no process in Singapore for a case to be reviewed after the appeal has been exhausted." As if all this were not enough, Martin actually heaped on a few extra duties for himself as the campaign headed into its final stretch.

Amongst the additional activities that Martin had taken on during the last week were the preparation for a final judicial challenge to the execution as well as a prayer session he was arranging to be held at Shanmugam's home the night before the execution.

Unlike his previous capital drug case, Martin did not have a local lawyer such as MG Guru assisting him. However, he did have two British lawyers, Messieurs Saul Lehrefreund, Parvais Jabbar and Edward Fitzgerald, Q.C. providing him with valuable long-distance support. Saul and Parvais had been alerted to the case and all its complications via Amnesty International. (Though the two gentlemen stress that they are not Amnesty lawyers per se.) They themselves have worked on many similar cases and are, in fact, specialists on the death penalty, having assisted in many cases involving the death penalty in the former British colonies of the Caribbean.

Saul and Parvais were able to carry out the important legal research on the issues that an already much over-stretched Martin would never have been able to carry out himself.

Not surprisingly, by the final week of the 'save-Shanmugam' campaign, Martin had come down with the flu. He had a high fever, his vision was blurred and he even occasionally had trouble simply walking. He knew that he should drag himself to a doctor, but he felt he couldn't take even that short amount of time away from the pursuit of the case. He needed to either be in his office, off consulting with those also fighting the execution, or ready to take an important call on his mobile phone. At the back of his mind was another worry: what if the doctor ordered him to bed for a few days? Those few days would bring him right to the time of the scheduled execution.

(In fact, he did manage during this time to call a doctor friend who told him he probably did belong in bed and was possibly endangering his health significantly by trying to ignore the flu. He thanked his friend and continued ignoring it.)

As exhausted as he was, as terrible as he felt, Martin had to turn down this possibility of a short recovery rest as he felt the fight was not yet over. Even if he felt deep down inside that the chances of success were close to zero, he needed to struggle to see the fight to the very end. He had only been getting three to five hours of sleep during this hectic fortnight, that had been squeezed into just two hours on the final two days.

Forty-eight hours before the scheduled execution, Martin called a last-minute press conference to announce one last judicial thrust. The press conference was held at the Oxford Hotel, a rather modest hotel on a quiet side street in the downtown area. The turnout included a number of non-press people who had followed the case for the previous few weeks. Amongst these was MG Guru, the ex-lawyer who had helped Martin in the preparations for the Vignes Mourthi hearings. The actual press representation was smaller, but did represent all the important press organisations here in the Lion City.

At this press conference, Martin called on the Singapore president to convene a constitutional court of three judges to rule on the constitutionality of the death penalty as the way it was administered in the Republic of Singapore. As Martin saw it, Article 12 of the constitution, which guarantees 'equal treatment and equality of the law", was being routinely violated in many death penalty cases. This was especially clear for Martin in Shanmugam's case, where he strongly felt his defendant had been denied this guaranteed equal treatment. The strong evidence for this, Martin pointed out, included those six cases cited in the clemency petition where the amount of drugs found was reduced to non-capital offence in reducing it to 499 grams

(500 grams attracks the death sentence). The president, predictably, refused to convene such a body.

At 3 a.m. on the morning of May 12th, Martin received a long-distance phone call from Saul and Parvais, the two lawyers assisting him from Britain. They gave him a run-down of all the research they had done which seemed pertinent to Shanmugam's case. Putting this all together, Martin decided he now had enough to take the matter into a court of law one more time. With the valuable assistance of those two lawyers in Britain, he had found his own procedure that he thought might yield some success in getting a stay of execution.

Then, less than one full day before the scheduled execution, shortly before noon, Martin filed an application in the court arguing that the essential principles of natural justice had been breeched in this case. Court officials said they would see what they could do to urgently find a judge to hear the argument. They, in fact, found a judge, and as luck would have it, it was Justice Lai Kew Chai, the 'sympathetic' justice from the Vignes Mourthi days. Coincidentally, the state was again represented by DPP Bala Reddy, from the Vignes Mourthi case.

By 3:30 p.m., Martin was standing in the High Court chamber before Judge Lai Kew Chai. The last-ditch session ran for three hours and was totally devoid of acrimony. Martin delivered his arguments for the first two hours; Martin's main argument was that the clemency process is defective in that it breaches the principles of natural justice. This is due to the fact that the President relies on the advice of the Cabinet who in turn relies on the opinion of the Attorney General. The Constitution that lays out this process is found in Article 22P. The Attorney Generals' Chambers is the body responsible for the Prosecution of Shanmugam and for the President and the

Cabinet to rely on the Attorney General's opinion on the issue of clemency conflicts with the rules of natural justice.

The President had turned down Martin's request to convene a Constitutional Court to address the various contraventions of the Constitution in Shanmugan's case.

Martin subsequently decided to complain to the United Nations Rapporteur for Extra-Judicial, Arbitrary and Summary Executions in asking them to intervene and stay the execution pending an inquiry into the constitutional issues that due process was not followed. Samydorai assisted Martin in filing the said complaint to the UN.

Martin also argued that the condemned prisoner must be allowed to see the reports by the judges (as prescribed under Article 22P) that were forwarded to the President. This is to ensure that the condemned prisoner can make an informed representation to the President, when the former files his clemency petition. To support his contention Martin cited various Commonwealth judgements which had similar constitutional challenges. This point had never been before the Singapore Courts.

DPP Reddy then countered with the state's case over the last hour. These proceedings were characterised by mutual respect between advocates and judge. However, the outcome was no more positive than what Martin had reaped in the three hearings on the Vignes Mourthi case.

Around 6:30 in the evening, Justice Lai peered sympathetically at an obviously exhausted Attorney Martin and announced that he was rejecting this last-ditch appeal. He said he would, in time, provide a written judgment setting down the grounds of Shanmugam's execution. As his client was not in the court with him at that point (in contrast to the final hearing for Vignes Mourthi), Martin quickly applied for a stay of execution so that the condemned man be allowed to read for himself the grounds of this specific judgement. Martin argued that this was simply Shanmugam's constitutional right - to read for himself the reasons why his final appeal was rejected.

Judge Lai also turned down this request, adding that the defence attorney could simply convey the grounds of the decision orally. Martin informed the court that since it was already 6:30pm, he would not have access to the prisoner, as the last visit was at 5pm.

As it happened, Martin never made it back to the prison that evening. Sam went to the gallows without ever having heard about the arguments presented on that last day or the grounds of Judge Lai's decision. However, he did have other, more important concerns to take care of now as he headed into his last hours. In fact, he apparently got very little or no sleep that final night.

Back at the prison, the condemned man and his family were preparing for what now seemed inevitable. His sister Mahes, who in recent years had been in many ways the family member closest to Shanmugam, visited him in the prison often. On her last visit to Changi, the day before the execution, the condemned man started crying. She said it was then that she fully realised the depth of his love for the family. By that point, he was also trying to work through a complicated knot of emotions.

At the end of his meeting with his sister, it was clear that the core fire of Sam's desire to live was still burning fiercely. Her older brother then entreated her to look after his two sons, his mother, her children - and herself. He then repeated this plea to Mahes second husband. (Her new husband was the last one to visit Sam, arriving about 4:10 and staying until the official end of visiting hours at 5 p.m.) The last words he ever said to his sister were, "I love you, Mahi." It was a simple expression of emotion, but behind the words,

Mahes feels she read something in his face that seemed to say, "Help me."

But Mahes simply had no idea how she could help this older brother who had helped her so often now that he so needed her. In fact, she could do little but cry to the guard. She then asked to be able to touch him, to hug him one more time before he was hanged. But this, of course, was against prison regulations, so the guard had to refuse her request.

(One of the saddest ironies of this story is that several years earlier, when Mahes herself was in an abyss of depression because of her marital problems, she had contemplated hanging herself. It was Shanmugam who sat down with her and talked her out of it, showing her all the reasons she had to go on living.)

Meet The Hangman

Although Singapore's stringent Official Secrets Act prevents Darshan Singh from talking about his job, an October 2005 article in The Australian newspaper revealed a number of interesting facts about Mr Singh's 46 years as the Lion City's principle hangman. In that time, Singh has personally dispatched some 850 condemned prisoners, including both Vignes Mourthi and Shanmugam Murugesu.

Singh replaced the British executioner, a Mr Seymour, back when Singapore was still a British colony. The then 27-year-old penal system officer actually volunteered for the hangman's post, enticed by the bonus pay involved. Today, the semi-retired Mr Singh draws 400 Singapore dollars for every execution he carries out.

Amongst the milestones in Singh's career as a hangman was the time he hanged 18 men in one day, in six rounds of three.

(This is believed to be a world record.) Those executed in this marathon gallows session in the early 1960's had all been convicted of leading a prisoner's uprising on a Singapore penal island which resulted in the deaths of four police officials.

Now a 73-year-old grandfather, Darshan Singh would like to pass along his grisly charge to someone else. But according to The Australian article (by veteran journalist Alan Shadrake), Singapore is having a hard time finding someone to fill Singh's shoes. A former colleague of Singh's claims that the affable hangman was grooming two successors, both of whom were members of the penal service. The two men had learned the mechanics of execution well enough, but when it came time to pull the lever for real prisoners, the two froze. Supposedly, one of the two trainees became so unsettled by the experience that he simply walked out and resigned from the penal service.

It is said that Singh's first wife also walked out - leaving him upon hearing the secret that he had kept from her for years; that he was Singapore's main

executioner. He now lives happily with his second wife and gets along well with their three adopted children. When one colleague asked him why he remained in this macabre job for so many years, Singh reportedly replied, "It's all I know. It has become my bread and butter."

But apparently, Singh is no cold-blooded sadist who delights in the hangings. He supposedly spends time with the condemned prisoners before the actual day of execution. He bestows special care and attention on those with few visitors or no religious support.

In the last moments of their lives, Singh reportedly fetters the condemned individuals' hands behind theirs back, then leads them on a short march to the gallows. After placing the rope securely around the prisoner's neck, Singh duly recites the hangman's words of solace: "I am going to send you to a better place than this. God bless you." Then, save for the short thump of a trap door opening, the rest is silence.

Mahes had also brought along her youngest child, then not quite eight months old, to the prison that day. Having been refused permission to touch Sam herself, she then implored the guard to at least let her condemned brother touch the baby, to confer his blessing upon the boy. However, this special request was also rejected. Rules are rules.

The next day, Sam's body was returned to the family. Finally, all those closest to him had ample opportunity to touch him. For a few hours at least. But at that point, Mahes no longer want to touch his body; her brother was dead, she could not touch him. She could only touch all the memories she now carried with her.

The prayer session arranged by the lawyer and held at Sam's own HDB flat on the evening of the 12th attracted between 20 and 30 people. The session consisted of diverse Hindu prayers and chants and ran for a good two hours. Most of the session was "spiritually charged", as at least one in attendance remembers it. Nonetheless, as it broke up, there was a sense of emotional and physical exhaustion amongst the participants.

Friday morning at 6 a.m, the family members directed their thoughts to Changi Prison. Like her brother, Mahes got almost no sleep that evening. After the prayer session, she had gone back to her own home to shower and take care of a few other matters, then returned to her mother's flat where Letchumi waited with Sam's two sons and his younger brother, Kuben. They were joined by one of their aunts.

Around 5:50, Mahes started to undergo some strange sensations. She felt as if her own head was being jerked upwards and her tongue came out. She started to feel pain course throughout her body. Seeing what was going on, her younger brother Kuben, the police officer, darted to her side; he tried to control her, to help her. She suddenly felt as if she herself were strangling, about to die. Her aunt, her mother's sister, rushed over with a glass of water. But the younger woman had trouble getting the water down; her aunt had to help her swallow it. Mahes today believes that if that aunt had not stepped in with the water, she might have joined her older brother that morning and died herself, right there in the flat.

The family had wanted some memento of Shanmugam in his last days and thought the best memento would be personal letters that he wrote during that time. An old friend, Brigitte, conveyed this wish to Sam on one of her last visits to the prison. Sam himself agreed that this might well be one of the most valuable legacies he could leave those closest to him. Consequently, he evidently did not sleep at all on the night of the 12th, his last night alive, but kept writing letter after letter, some long, some short, to various people. He continued with this task all the way up through the early hours of the morning, when his sad journey was brought to an end.

After his death, prison officials handed over letters written in that last night to Shanmugam's mother, two sons and others. However, there were no letters passed to his sister Mahes and her children. This was odd, as he had been so close to his sister and quite fond of his niece and nephew. In fact, Mahes had expressly asked her brother to write a missive that she could carry with her as a last memory of the man who had done so much for her. However, the prison officials maintained that no letter had been left behind for either her or her children. For his sister, this remains the final mystery of the Shanmugam Murugesu case.

The funeral ceremonies took place late that afternoon, in the home of Letchumi, where Sam's two boys had lived since their father's arrest and where Sam himself had lived briefly after the break-up of his marriage. Cremation followed at the massive Mandai Crematorium at the far end of the island. The

Hindu prayers at the ceremony were recited by lawyer R. Martin and by V. A. Sivakumar, the publisher of the Hindu website who had been stopped from speaking at the vigil a week earlier. The attendance at this ceremony was much larger than at Vignes' send-off, with a significant number of Singaporean citizens and residents turning out for the rites. If for no other reason, the people who had been behind the campaign to save Shanmugam could claim some small victory here. Finally, people in the Island Republic were starting to get concerned about these issues. Perhaps the next time, the victory would not be just a moral victory.

Deterring - Who, How and When

A large number of countries across the globe still retain the death penalty, though each of these countries has its own roster of crimes that merit the ultimate punishment. For instance, adultery can be a capital offence in quite a few countries around the world, while in other death penalty lands it's considered more of a competitive sport.

Britain, which effectively abolished the death penalty in 1965, at one time recognised a grand total of 223 capital crimes - including that frightening transgression of "breaking down the head or mound of any fishpond". In practice, however, only 25 of these offences actually resulted in execution for the perpetrators. And for hundreds of years, these hangings (and earlier, the beheadings) were public spectacles.

Indeed, public hangings were extremely popular events in 18th century London, often drawing up to 200,000 spectators at one go. These 'shows' were performed mainly at an open field called Tyburn Gallows, the present site of Marble Arch in central London. The open-air executions continued there until 1783, when they were moved to Newgate Prison.

While the authorities did not charge a fee to attend the executions (they were supposed to serve as cautionary lessons to those watching them), well-to-do British gentlemen and ladies would dole out handsome sums for a prime seat in the stands immediately facing the gallows. These seats were known as Mother Proctor's Pews, named for the enterprising lady who owned them and who apparently made a good living off the dying. During the executions, other business-minded types would ply the huge crowds selling snacks or hawking broadsides.

Throughout most of the 18th century, there were five to eight hanging days a year at Tyburn, which roughly corresponded with the eight Assize Sessions at the Old Bailey. The huge crowds would gather and follow the execution processions as they made their way out to Tyburn for the actual hangings.

The multiple-drop gallows at Tyburn consisted of three tall uprights joined at the top with triangular-shaped beams. Under each of these beams, three carts could be lined up at a time, each holding eight prisoners. Thus, the gallows (which bore the nicknames 'the triple tree' or 'the deadly nevergreen') was capable of dispatching up to 24 miscreants at a time. On a good show day for the spectators, they would.

It is estimated that throughout the 18th century, the heyday of Enlightenment England, some 3,000 male prisoners were publicly executed at Tyburn. Reliable records tell us that there were also 182 women hanged there during this period. But even though women executionees were somewhat rare, amongst the biggest 'draws' for the hangings were some of England's most notorious female convicts.

One of the most celebrated of the women convicts who met her end at Tyburn was Mary Young, better known under her professional name of Jenny Diver. "Diver" was 18th century slang for pickpocket, which was this very talented lady's specialty. Jenny, or Mary, had been arrested and sentenced to forced emigration and labour in the American colonies at least twice before being ordered to 'dance at the Tyburn tree'. Apparently, long before American baseball was invented, London judges had adopted the principle of "three strikes and you're out".

Under her professional name of Jenny Diver, Mary has come down to us through history via John Gay's famous musical, The Beggar's Opera, as well as The Threepenny Opera, the Kurt Weill-Bertolt Brecht updating of this classic 18th century comic opera. Both of these shows focus on the gangster boss MacHeath, who has a special fondness for his col-

league, Jenny Diver.

In fact, one major irony surrounding these executions was that the food, drink and broadside vendors weren't the only small businesspeople working the crowds that came to view the hangings. Numerous eyewitness accounts mention that pickpockets often turned up for the events, and had a field day with folks busy ogling the executions - even when those executed were themselves pickpockets. Both Daniel Defoe (of Robinson Crusoe fame) and Dr. Samuel Johnson remarked on this phenomenon.

The liberal-minded Defoe cited this fact as evidence that hanging was not a deterrent to crime, as the ultimate punishment certainly didn't keep the pickpockets away. More ardent law-and-order types took issue with Defoe, arguing that if London's 'divers' hadn't been so harshly dealt with, there would have been three to five times as many pickpockets working those oh-so-enticing crowds watching the hangings.

It is a strange, somewhat macabre custom for Changi Prison Services to do a "photo shoot" with condemned prisoners approximately 24 hours before they are to be executed.

Ostensibly for the benefit of the family, the condemned man is depicted in thirteen or so everyday poses as if a model in a photo shoot; smiling and sitting behind a desk – as though a "company manager", dressed in a suit, etc. This photo was handed over to Madam Letchumi after the execution. It hangs on the wall of Madam Letchumi Murugesu's living room. She sleeps beneath it every night.

REPUBLIC OF SINGAPORE
CERTIFICATE OF REGISTRATION OF DEATH

DEATH REGISTRATION NO

583079 F

Death registered at	CHANGI NPC

DECEASED

Full name of deceased	SHANMUGAM S/O S MURUGESU		
NRIC/Identification Document No.	S1741586G	Sex	MALE

Date of birth	24/11/1966

Race/Dialect Group	INDIAN / TAMIL	
Nationality	SINGAPORE CITIZEN	
Country of birth	SINGAPORE	

Home Address: APT BLK 93 HENDERSON ROAD #02-206 SINGAPORE 150093

Date and hour of death: 13/05/2005 0606

Place or Address where death occurred: 982 UPPER CHANGI ROAD NORTH S(507709) SINGAPORE

CAUSE OF DEATH BY CERTIFIER

Approximate interval between onset and death

	Years	Months	Days	Hours
I Disease or Condition leading to death (a) FRACTURE DISLOCATION OF CERVICAL SPINE S(507709)	INSTANTANEOUS			
(b)				
Antecedent Causes (c)				
II Other Significant conditions				

Name and official status of person certifying cause of death: DR NORKHALIM DALIL, MEDICAL PRACTITIONER

Certificate of Cause of Death Reference No.: N 020565
Date: 13/05/2005

INFORMANT

Name: ANG LING DAR

Address: 982 UPPER CHANGI ROAD NORTH S(507709)

NRIC/Identification Document No.: 00502

Relationship: RO

I certify that the above information given by me is correct.

Informant's Signature/Thumb impression — 13/5/05 Date

REGISTRATION OFFICER

Name of Registration Officer: HOE MING SHEN

Designation: REGISTRATION OFFICER

Date: 13/05/2005

for Registrar of Birth and Deaths

DISPOSITION

PERMIT TO BURY/CREMATE BODY [The Environment Public Health Act (Chapter 95)]

Place of Burial
or
Place of Cremation: MANDAI CREMATORIUM

Religious type: HINDU

INFORMANT MAKING APPLICATION

I ANG LING DAR

NRIC/Identification Document No 00502 apply for a permit to
☐ bury + ☑ cremate +
the deceased referred to in the Death Certificate No. **583079 F**
For application to cremate only
☐ I certify that to the best of my knowledge, the deceased has no written direction that he/she should not be cremated +

Informant's Signature/Thumb impression — 13/5/05 Date

REGISTRATION OFFICER

The Certificate of Cause of Death certified that there is
☑ No evidence of pacemaker in the body of the deceased +
☐ Evidence of pacemaker/device removed from the body of the deceased +
Permit is approved.

13/05/2005
Date

CHANGI NPC
9 SIMEI STREET 2
SINGAPORE 529914

CHANGI NPC
for Commissioner of Public Health

197

Chapter 13

AFTERMATHS

Everything should be as simple as it is, but not simpler.

- Albert Einstein

A lawyer can become just like a part of the family and feel the loss of the executed prisoner as deeply as some of the family. I know this feeling because I myself, M Ravi, have twice suffered such a terrible sense of loss when my clients went to the gallows. Those two clients were the men you have just read about in this book - Shanmugam Murugesu and Vignes Mourthi.

A you may have guessed by now, R. Martin is M.Ravi who took on both of these emotion-wrenching cases at the eleventh hour after all appeals had been closed. If some of the insights about the lawyer and his knowledge of his clients seemed quite close-focus, it was because I was there.

For this book, I've chosen to adopt a third-person form of narrative up to this point for a few reasons. For one thing, I didn't want the reader to think that the person telling the story had a heavy axe to grind and was using the tale to either aggrandize or justify himself. I have long thought that the stories spoke for themselves and did not need any zealous editorialising on my part.

By writing the book with a third-person narrative, I was also able to crawl out of my own skin a little and look at the story from a more objective vantage point. I actually began to see some things in a way I had not done before.

I was, as you can imagine, deeply committed to both of my clients and their plights during the course of my defending them and even afterwards.

However, while writing from the slightly removed third-person perspective, I think I have brought in an element of objectivity that allowed me to present the cases even more convincingly. I have not changed my mind about the issues of capital punishment in general or the execution of these two men. In fact, I'm now even more strengthened in my convictions having, as it were, stepped back and looked at the cases from another viewpoint.

Finally, we decided the third-person narrative was the most reader-friendly way of presenting these two very real stories. They both contain rich dramas that should not be reduced to dry legal documents and bloodless transcripts of trials and hearings. By giving you a third-person narrator here, I hope I have been an even more effective guide through the stories. (For some strange reasons, people tend to trust the third-person narrator in such stories more than they do someone who was right in the thick of the battle.)

I was there, front and centre, for these fights (in the final stages at least) and felt all the ups and downs, the fears and hopes, the warmth of supporters and the cold grip of judicial logic that filled them. I'd like to think that in presenting the stories to you the way I did, I made it even easier for you to make that journey right along with me. If so, I have succeeded in almost everything I wanted to achieve with this book. Thank you for coming along with me.

Media's adverse publicity stunt

In addition to the clients I lost as a result of my involvement in the Vignes Mourthi and Shanmugam's case, the Singapore media continue to aggressively pursue an adverse publicity campaign against me that has led to more clients leaving me fearing they would face adverse decicions in court as result of engaging me as their attorney. One of the recent reports in a leading newspaper even highlighted that my late father was an alcoholic and my late mother had committed suicide . It is not surpising that Singapore had clinched the 147th place in press freedom among the countries in the list and the Singapore media continues to be proud of that.

Complaints after Complaints

I had a number of complaints lodged against me with the local Law Society from September 2003 through November of that year - the same period wherein I was trying to get Vignes Mourthi's case reversed or in the immediate aftermath of that campaign.

To be precise, the roster of complaints started in the week after I actually filed the Criminal Motion in the High Court on behalf of Vignes. Here were the six complaints that I was forced to deal with:

1) On 8 September, I visited visited Changi Women's Prison to interview a client. However, my entry was delayed by prison authorities. This led to a disagreement. A complaint was filed at the Law Society against me by the authorities.

Outcome: . I received a reprimand from the Law Society gazetted to be published, and was ordered to pay $3,000 in legal costs to the Law Society.

2) Judge Woo Bih Li filed a complaint to the Law Society against me because of what he saw as unacceptable behaviour in his court during the first hearing on the Vignes Mourthi case. This centred on the exchange we had had during the tense moments in that hearing.

Outcome: I received a $500 fine.

3) District Judge Wong Chun Ngee lodged a complaint against me because of certain exchanges we had at a mention on 15th October 2003.

Outcome: A disciplinary hearing on this matter is still pending as of August 2005 and I face the prospect of suspension.

4) A further complaint was lodged against me by District Judge Kow Keng Siong because of what transpired at a mention on 15 October. This mention stemmed from the incidents at Changi Women's Prison . At this session, I informed the court that I was denied access to my client and intended to apply for Judicial Review. This involved not only the two incidents in early September, but a letter the prison authorities had sent me on 15 September claiming that my client found me unsuitable and no longer wished to engage my firm on the case. I highlighted that my client confirmed at a trial in the Court on 22 September 2003 September 2003 that she continued to engage me as her counsel.(That trial was fixed for 5 days between 22 September 2003 to 26th September 2003. My request to adjourn the trial was turned down by Judge Tay Yong Kwang who was also the trial judge for Vignes Mourthy's case.)

Judge Kow himself claimed that I had made an application without taking instructions from my client there in the prison. I strongly pointed out that he had misunderstood the action and that it did not directly involve my client but myself being denied access to my own client wherein my rights had been trampled with.

Outcome: I had to pay a $1,000 fine.

5) I was arrested for "disorderly behaviour" at a pub near the popular Clarke's Quay area following a shouting match with police officers sent to

deal with an unruly acquaintance of mine who called me for legal advice on that night. I called the Police for assistance fearing my safety when there was an altercation and a scuffle erupted between the bouncers and the acquaintance but ironically I was arrested and charged in court.

Outcome: I was briefly detained and eventually had to pay a $700 fine.

6) Finally there was a complaint to the Law Society lodged against me by 2 senior lawyers in Singapore.

Outcome : Complaint dismissed

This marked the end of the complaints .

The price I was forced to pay for these complaints could be measured in both time and money. I had to attend to each inquiry as it came, and I represented myself in the subsequent hearings, save for the last two hearings. As if all these were not enough,The Law Society of Singapore called for my files under a section of the Legal Professions Act. As I had transferred operations from my Buena Vista office after the Vignes Mourthi's case, I also had the unenviable task of running all around to locate the relevant files.

As it happened, the files and the accounts were generally found to be in order. However, I did have to fork out $5,500 to pay my accountants for their extra work on this.

An Offer He Had To Refuse

Shanmugam had been suspended as a taxi driver by the CityCab firm when he was arrested. This is apparently company policy. Then, on 26 July 2005, he received a letter from his former taxi company inviting him to return to the taxi force. Unfortunately, having been executed two and a half months earlier, Shanmugam was unable to accept this thoughtful invitation.

Songs for Sam

A pair of rock concerts were held at the Substation in memory of Shanmugam on 5 and 18 August 2005. Organised by a group of artists and others called Songs for Sam, the concerts featured local bands and speeches by different parties, including mine, who spoke about the ordeal of mounting the final defence for Shanmugam. Recalling the problems connected with the vigil, where the police had notified the organisers beforehand that they probably would not get a license for an outdoor presentation, this licensed event was held in the Substation's Guinness Theatre, an indoor venue.

The concerts were conceived as both a memorial tribute to Shanmugam and the start of an ongoing series of concerts, projects and events across the region against the death penalty.

The only objection that the police authorities had with this show was with the posters advertising the concerts. Their concern with the posters was that they had pictures of Sam on them. This was considered a "glorification" of a convicted felon. Accordingly, a police spokesman called up one of the show's organisers and told him that all posters and placards containing images of Sam had to be taken down. The organisers duly complied and the concerts went ahead with no other interference except there were numerous police in plain clothes.

"An Attempt to Subvert the Course of Justice"

Sgt Rajkumar was, you'll recall, the prosecution's most valuable witness in the Vignes Mourthi case. Not only was he the man who applied the sting in the first arrest, it was his testimony that sealed Vignes' fate. The controversial P40 piece of evidence - the snippet from the sergeant's field book which quoted the defendant as replying, "It's very good. You watch and see. You are sure to come back to deal with me again" to the undercover agent's consumer inquiry about the quality of whatever that plastic bag held - just about sealed the case against the younger man. If you accepted this bit of evidence, it's almost undeniable that Vignes knew what he was handing over.

But, as mentioned in Chapter 3, the sergeant entered that bit of evidence into his field book some time after the actual arrest. And we have since discovered that between those two dates, the officer had some other serious concerns of his own that may have twisted his memory a tad.

On 21 September 2001 - one day after the double arrests in Woodlands - Sgt. Rajkumar took a young woman of his acquaintance to a friend's apartment. There he reportedly handcuffed her and, while she was handcuffed, had anal sex with the woman before returning home to his dear wife, at that point three months pregnant.

Rajkumar has always insisted that the sex was consensual. The young woman in question has not always been of the same opinion. The day after this encounter at his friend's home, the woman filed rape and sodomy charges against the police officer. (Sodomy, defined as anal sex, is here in the Lion City a criminal offence even between consenting adults. For that matter, oral sex between consenting adults can also be classified as a crime.)

Rajkumar was himself arrested on these charges on 23 September, a Sunday. He, of course, avowed his innocence and was duly released on bail.

Within a short period of time - co-terminal with the drug arrests interrogations - a swarm of the sergeant's friends launched into an intensive public relations campaign with the young woman on his behalf. They told her about his pregnant wife, his ailing father and his suicidal mother. (In one account, the friends claimed that the officer's mother had tried to throw herself from a parapet on hearing of his arrest on rape charges.)

They also told this young woman that if the case were brought to court, her own somewhat extensive sexual past would be brought up and given full play in the press. This would not only hurt her relationship with her current boyfriend, but would also most likely bring great shame upon her family. (This kind of intimidation masked as friendly advice was also just plain inaccurate: in Singapore, the identities of alleged victims in rape cases are carefully guarded. The names, ethnic backgrounds and sometimes even the ages of victims are kept out of all press accounts and even the official court records.)

A former close friend of Rajkumar's, Alex, became the key witness for the prosecution. Alex, described by the judge in his written verdict as "a simple and truthful witness" asked the sergeant if he had in fact handcuffed and sodomized the woman. According to Alex, Rajkumar admitted that he had, but he was only following her request in doing so. Rajkumar also told Alex that he would not admit this to his own lawyer because he "had seen many such cases in court and he was afraid his lawyer might not fight the case for him if he admitted to this."

These friends also offered the alleged victim monetary rewards if she would go back to the police and retract her statements, thus dropping all charges against their friend. The promised sums amounted to $10,500, including a very favourable $500 loan she received: a loan without any interest or discussion or repayment. (The judge later aptly referred to this loan as "merely a euphemism for the money given" to persuade the young woman to retract her statement to the police). As there apparently was also some evidence of anal penetration, the young lady was urged to blame this on some fictional 'foreigner' who could no longer be found. Just tell the police that the sodomy was with this foreigner and not with Sergeant Rajkumar, she was advised by the officer's friends.

Rajkumar has always maintained that his friends did this on their own initiative and that he had even angrily warned them on several occasions not to get involved in this way. (As it is a crime to thus influence a witness to withdraw charges.) He says he was always champing at the bit to go up against this woman in open court, as they had already engaged in sex on various occasions, and this particular job was just another incidence of their consensual coupling.

However, the public prosecutor just didn't buy this story. The convenience of the young woman's retraction did, in fact, arouse suspicions and Rajkumar and one of his friends, Balbir Singh, were indicted on grounds of violating the Prevention of Corruption Act. (A local way of saying they were suspected of having suborned a witness in a serious criminal case).

A string of witnesses on both sides took the stand in his corruption trial. Ultimately, on 31 March 2005, Rajkumar and his friend were both found guilty by District Court Judge Sia Aik Kor on the corruption charges. The judge was just not swayed by either Rajkumar's testimony or that of his witnesses. He agreed with the prosecution's witnesses that the officer had put his friends up to the bribery and even paid some of them back for their actions. The veteran policeman was clever enough not to offer the young woman the bribes and enticements himself. That would have been much too obvious. But he had encouraged his friends to do it for him, the judge ruled.

As a result of this verdict, Rajkumar was sentenced to 15 months in prison, Balbir Singh to 6 months. The rape and sodomy charges against the now former police officer are still pending as of this writing.

Ironically, the sergeant's co-defendant, Mr Singh, who had likewise been a police officer for seven years at the time of his arrest, complained of the methods used during his interrogation by the police. This was, in fact, the cornerstone of his whole defence: that incriminating statements he signed while in police custody had been involuntarily squeezed out of him.

In particular, he cited the fact that his first signed statement was only inked after he had been forced to go almost two days without sleep, had been interrogated in an exceedingly cold room, had developed a severe migraine, and when the interrogating officer threatened to keep him another 48 hours if he refused to sign. A second statement was signed under trickery, Singh claimed; the interrogators had slipped him a page which they said was an unsigned portion from the earlier statement and asked him to sign this page, which he did without reading.

These claims bore sharp echoes of the case presented by Vignes Mourthi's defence team: that certain incriminating statements were signed because Vignes was worn-out after gruelling interrogations and did not pay full attention to every single point in the statement he was admitting to. And, of course, one of Vignes' interrogators was that very Sergeant Rajkumar, whose problems with a particular young lady had initiated this whole process on corruption charges.

More to the point, the same S. Rajkumar whose contested testimony had conclusively nailed Vignes Mourthi was later found guilty of "...actions so obviously corrupt by the ordinary and objective standard that he must know his conduct is corrupt" in Judge Sia Aik Kor's words. The judge also cited a precedent which found actions such as those undertaken by Rajkumar to be "..akin to an attempt to subvert the course of justice". And we should keep in mind that all of these criminal actions occurred at pretty much the same time that Sergeant Rajkumar of the Central Narcotics Bureau was playing a central role in preparing the state's air-tight case against Vignes Mourthi.

Appendix I

THE OFFICIAL SECRETS ACT

Regrettably, there are a number of gaps or omissions in this book. The reason for these gaps is that the author and researcher were restricted both in where they could go in telling the story as well as in their use of certain materials.

For instance, we had to employ pseudonyms for some of those in the legal profession who appear in the book. We were also compelled to use some information as 'deep background', but not include it in the final text. These two tactics were imposed upon us by Singapore's stringent libel laws, which grant considerable protection to those in the public sphere who get written about.

But an even more regrettable choice forced upon us was the decision not to pursue such questions as the last hours of the three men executed here, what they may have said to warders in their last moments, and certain aspects of the police investigations and judicial processes. The reason for these omissions is Singapore's rigorous Official Secrets Act.

Most of the provisions of the Official Secrets Act do seem quite reasonable, necessary even, so as to protect the safety and vital interests of Singapore and all those living here. It prohibits the making or receiving of any photographs, drawings, sketches, designs, models (or the like) of any military installations, military vehicles, weapons, etc. It also specifically prohibits making or passing along photos, drawings, sketches or designs of railway lines, bridges, ports, air travel facilities, etc - all those places that make such tempting targets for terrorists or foreign enemies.

(Anyone officially authorised to take photographs or make drawings of non-sensitive areas of these places for advertising, publicity, books, articles, etc. are exempted from prosecution under this act. But such individuals must apply for a permit.)

The main problem for journalists, authors, and artists arises with the broad interpretation of the term "safety and interests of Singapore". In our case, for instance, talking to certain police officers about the arrests and interrogations or to prison officials or the hangmen about the details of the incarceration, the specific executions or the demeanour and attitudes of the prisoners in their last moments could be declared 'against the interests of Singapore' and thus a criminal offence. Not only would we be guilty of violating the law for soliciting and publishing such information, but those on the inside who provided the information to us would also be guilty of a similar crime.

The penalties for violating this act can be quite stiff. If anyone publishes anything considered to be in contravention of the law, all those involved can be fined $2,000 (Singapore dollars) and sentenced to a prison term of up to 2 years. More significantly perhaps, all proscribed materials would have to be returned - which in the case of a book would mean all copies would need to be withdrawn (insofar as possible) and the offending passages excised before the book could go back on the market.

Further, any individual who works in a company which has been involved in violating any provisions of this act (for example, my law office) could be called in to prove that he or she was not involved in any way in making those official secrets public.

The two of us involved in the research of this book could also have been declared guilty of a crime for merely soliciting or attempting to persuade those people on the inside to give us any information protected by this law. One ominous sentence in the statute alludes to the guilt of anyone who "aids or abets or does any act preparatory to the commission of an offence under this Act" and goes on to say that any such person "shall be guilty of an offence and shall be liable on conviction to the same punishment, and to be proceeded against in the same manner, as if he had committed the offence" (emphasis added).

Faced with the possible penalties for ourselves and others if we had gone forth and tried to penetrate the shield of secrecy in these areas, we decided to let our discretion be the better part of valour. We know there were tiny, dark corners that could have been explored very beneficially in telling the full story here, but the current structure of the law designates these areas as strict no-go zones.

Appendix II

VISIT TO CHANGI PRISON, THURSDAY 12 MAY 2005

by Lucy Davis

(This is an edited version of an email circulated on the Singapore arts community e-group immediately after the writer returned from a visit to Changi prison and the day before Shanmugam Murugesu's execution. Lucy Davis, one of the organisers of the vigil at the Furama Hotel, became very engaged in the campaign against the death penalty and has since forged strong bonds with Shanmugam's family)

I finally got permission to visit Shanmugam Murugesu--his friends call him "Sam"--in Changi today. I hadn't wanted to go, but his sister insisted I do so and so I couldn't say no. Now I'm very glad that I did.

I went in to see Sam at the same time as his mother, Madam Letchumi, who was already in the visiting cell, and together with Lynn, one of his best female friends from wake-boarding. Only two friends went to visit Sam on his last day, both females. "Sam was a 'girl's best friend' kind of guy," they said.

The exterior of the Changi Prison Link Centre looks most of all like an airport lounge, all glass and steel with huge designer-typographic letters on the outside. You enter through glass doors and are immediately asked by the guards what you are doing there and who you are there to see, before being ushered over to the registration counter, where you give in your IC or passport. You are then given a key to a locker and asked to remove all hard objects, such as jewellery, before entering

I had written Sam a long letter with all sorts of photos and pictures.

These were all ceremoniously ripped off before the letter itself was, I hope, accepted. It disappeared with one of the guards. The blown-up photocopies of Sam, his twin boys as babies, and his family that we had put together for the vigil were also rejected as they were not regulation size--the prison only accepts 3R images. The flowers I brought from my garden to show Sam were also thrown in the trash.

There aren't that many people in the cold, brand-new waiting hall, just small clusters of family members quietly huddled here and there, some crying, some eating their packed lunches, most waiting and waiting. Some relatives of people who have already been executed also come to the waiting hall on the Thursday prior to an execution to support the family of the person whose turn it is to go. There was a Malay lady there whose son had been hung in early April and another man whose son had been hung later that same month.

After a short wait, Lynn and I were ushered through turnstiles and down, down an endless white tunnel towards the max security section--kind of like the aeroplane tubes at Changi or Charles de Gaulle Airport, only with lower ceilings, narrower passages going on forever and ever and then suddenly plunging down narrow staircases. It was like architects had designed the place using one hand of Kafka, another of Escher. It was like we were the ones descending into hell.

The experience at Changi was all the more eerie as there was a power failure the day of our visit. It was hot and there were no lights and we had to find our way through the labyrinth via dim, neon torchlights held by guards posted along the route.

We walked silently, together with a group of Malay aunties who were also going to visit their relative--also one of the death row inmates. From afar, we must have looked like something from a late Medieval painting, so dark and dreamlike through the gloom.

But when we reached the entrance to the high security section, the scene was more like an episode of the TV show Alias, with laser-beam security and a whole series of even more metal turnstiles.

It struck me how such an "excess" of concrete steel, violence, security personnel and even poetics (the atmosphere, the architecture) was deemed necessary to keep the soft fragile bodies of only nine men in check.

The room itself where Sam was waiting with his mother was airless and tiny. Sam's friend raced in front of us and opened the door first. The glass was smeared with handprints and kiss marks and the wall underneath the window was black from the soles of many frustrated shoes.

The family will not be permitted to hug their son before he goes. The first time they will get to touch him is when his broken body comes back home from the gallows to be bathed.

Sam is a lovely, gentle regular guy. He reminds me mostly of my brother and the wake-board crowd he used to hang out with at Punggol. He is also handsome. His hair and beard were well kept. He was dressed in a white prison T-shirt, with his number 859. He was, of course, paler than in the photos from when he was a jet ski champion or the dreamy, happy ones from his holiday in India with his girlfriend that we have seen in the e-mails.

He was crying—not really out of fear, but because he had to say goodbye forever to all his family and friends. He kept one hand pressed throughout to the glass on the other side of where the hand of his friend was placed and one hand to his mother's while all three silently wept. He wanted his Mother to stop crying, but she couldn't.

He asked whether any more of his friends would be coming to visit him.

We had to tell him "No". He asked his friend about her golden retriever, whether she still spoils him. He told her she had to promise to keep going out and having fun. He told her he could see her partying away at 60. He repeated again: "I love you so much, I wish I could take you with me".

(Brigitte, the other friend who was there that day, told me how Sam used to take her dog for rides in his yellow jeep and she would see them coming down the road, heads turned to each other, conversing. She also told me how they used to watch TV together wearing cosmetic face masks, and how Sam used to get his jeep and follow his boys around after school, watching them in secret as they played football, just to check they were okay and not getting into mischief).

I told Sam that so many, people would be watching out for his family and his two boys and that people were thinking of him all over the world.

Sam asked after Ravi, his lawyer. I told him that Ravi loved him very much, but that he was putting through an eleventh-hour appeal to the High Court that day--which wasn't going to work, but he had to try. I said that Ravi might not be able to visit him and say goodbye. He looked very sad at this and said Ravi was a very brave, very good man.

Sam also said how very grateful he is for all of your support and everything you have done for his family. He also told his other friend earlier in the day that he read one letter from what he thought was a twelve-year-old boy, written to him during the vigil. He said that this letter really touched him, expressed as it was in a child's language, but still trying to grapple with the gravity of the thing.

The female guard then came and told us our time was up. We all three pressed our hands against the glass saying we knew we would see each other again. The guards had to ask us several times before we finally had to let go.

Appendix III

PRESS RELEASE - PLEA TO SAVE NGUYEN

by M.Ravi

1. Shanmugam Murugesu was executed in May of this year on Friday the 13th, which we recall as a black day for Singapore despite a high profile campaign by the civil society in Singapore and also despite my application in Court which was heard 12 hours before the execution and also asking the President to convene a Constitutional Court on the potential breaches of the Constitution, a request which was turned town.

2. Shanmugam, a national athlete who brought fame for Singapore, had on occasions when I met him in the prison, made a personal appeal to me to do all the best to campaign to save Nguyen Tuong Van's ("Van") life. He also mentioned that he was the confidante for Van during his time in the prison and would express to me that the feeling among the guys on death row was that if any of them were to get off they would be glad if it was Van, as he was so "very young and a soft-spoken soul". Shanmugam also said that even if Shanmugam's life was not spared that I should continue to fight to save this young man's life.

3. The President had turned down the clemency plea for Van. It came as a surprise to me, given the recent negotiations between the Singapore and Australian Governments on the issue of extraditing Mc Crea to Singapore.

Discrimination under Article 12(a) of the Constitution, equal treatment and equality before law

Discrimination in Singapore

4. The fact that in Mc Crea's case the Singapore Executive had given an undertaking that Mc Crea will not be executed even if he is convicted of murder is an indication that the Executive had exercised discretion on the issue of capital punishment. This was even before Mc Crea's trial had begun.

5. We have been arguing in Singapore that there should be Judicial discretion in capital cases and most importantly in drug-related cases when the burden of proof is reversed on the accused. The reason being an overwhelming number of executions are related to drugs trafficking. The Singapore Executive had even gone one step further to say that they will advise the President on clemency.

6. Even before Mc Crea's case begins, the Government had given undertaking. Therefore an Executive discretion had been exercised vis-a-vis Judicial discretion. Even if Mc Crea, who is alleged to have committed double murder, is convicted, he will not get a death sentence. That is the essence of the undertaking of the Singapore Government as far as his case is concerned. If the courts were to pass death sentence, the President would then grant clemency.

7. If the Government had decided to exercise discretion, why are judges prevented in exercising judicial discretion. Judicial discretion is more en-

dearing by constitutional standards and endures within the realm of the rule of law. Hence, Van is treated unequally on the issue of clemency against the backdrop of Mc Crea's case. Therefore, Article 12 is invoked in favour of Van in that he is treated unequally before the law and thereby discriminated against under Singapore's Constituion.

In PP v Taw Chen Kong, the Chief Justice quoted the Privy Council case of Ong Ah Chuan v PP, where Lord Diplock succinctly states the equality provision.

"Equality before the law and equal protection of the law require that like should be compared with like. What Article 12 (1) of the Constitution assures to the individual is the right to equal treatment with other individuals in similar circumstances."

Discrimination in Australia

8. The fact that the foreign ministry in Australia said that the due process had been followed is flawed and shows their discriminatory attitude to Van's case. Both cases spring forth from Australia - one is a British national who resided in Australia and the other is an Australian citizen of Vietnamese origin. To further elaborate on the point: I would argue that the Australian Foreign Ministry's comment of " the due process is followed" is also discriminatory to Van under the Australian Constitution when it is plain and obvious that the very Foreign Ministry which canvassed for Mc Crea shut a blind eye to Van on this point of equality before the Constitution.

9. It is inspiring as an anti-death penalty citizen to note the fervour of

the Australians on this issue to save Van from being executed, when all legal avenues are seemingly closed. There were constitutional arguments raised before the Australian Courts on Mc Crea's case, on the issue of extradition and the death penalty. It is up to the Constitutional experts in Australia to explore and advise their government on this issue of discrimination. But certainly, I would like to highlight this issue to Amnesty International Australia and the Australian Coalition Against Death Penalty. What is sauce for the goose is sauce for the gander. But Mc Crea's case is source on the issue of discrimination as far as the clemency process issue of Van is concerned.

Article 22(P) of the Singapore Constitution – Nguyen Tuong Van suffers a breach of the principle of natural justice

10. The President's refusal to grant a pardon to the applicant be set aside by way of an application in court or Petition to the President to reconsider his decision. This is based on the ground that the Presidential pardon process under Article 22P of the Constitution contravenes the principles of natural justice and further contravenes Article 9(1) of the Constitution, and the execution of the application should be stayed or set aside pending the determination on this issue. The essence of the aforesaid is that article 22(P) itself is in breach of the principles of natural justice because the decision-making process involving the pardon is defective as the President's decision when exercising judgement whether to grant a pardon in a particular case is based on the Attorney General's opinion. Hence Article 22(P) contravenes Article 9(1) which says "No person shall be deprived of his life or personal liberty save in accordance with law". Accordance with law means principles of natural justice are observed.

The whole of Article 22P is reproduced below :

Grant of pardon, etc. 22P.

(1) The President, as occasion shall arise, may, on the advice of the Cabinet

(2) Where any offender has been condemned to death by the sentence of any court and in the event of an appeal such sentence has been confirmed by the appellate court, the President shall cause the reports which are made to him by the Judge who tried the case and the Chief Justice or other presiding Judge of the appellate court to be forwarded to the Attorney-General with instructions that, after the Attorney-General has given his opinion thereon, the reports shall be sent, together with the Attorney-General's opinion, to the Cabinet so that the Cabinet may advise the President on the exercise of the power conferred on him by clause (1).

11. It is crystal clear that there has been a breach of the principles of natural justice as the decision-making process of the pardon is defective in the exercise of the President's refusal to grant pardon. Also, the special reports by judges forwarded to the Cabinet,AG or President are not disclosed and made available to the condemned prisoner to present his Clemency petition. The non-disclosure of the reports to the condemned prisoner is also a breach of natural justice. Annexed herewith is a copy of my affidavit supporting the aforesaid contention which was filed in Court in Shanmugam's case.

President is empowered under Article 100 of the Constitution to convene a Constitutional Court on any issue relating to the Constitution

12. I am urging the President in my capacity as a citizen to convene a Constitutional Court in view of the aforesaid breaches of the Constitution in Van's case. It is open to the people of Singapore to likewise ask the President to convene a Constitutional Court on an urgent basis so that then "the due process is followed" before rushing into this execution. I also appeal to the Australians to urge the President to do so.

13. I am submitting my Petition to the President through this Press Conference and the said Petiton will be served on the President by today, a copy of which is enclosed herewith.

14. I respectfully urge that his Excellency treat the matter with urgency given the nature of the Petition. If a reply is not forthcoming by the President by Tuesday,31 October 2005, I wish to place his Excellency on notice that I will proceed to file a complaint to the United Nations Special Rappoteur for Extra-Judicial,Summary or Arbitrary Executions on the aforesaid manifest breaches on due process in pleading with the UN to urge the Singapore authorities to stay the execution pending an inquiry by the UN on the aforesaid matters and also urge the UN to appeal to the President to conveve a Constitutional Court to address the contravention of the Constitution.

15. I appeal to the Australian public to take this matter on an urgent basis to the United Nations. As my resources are limited, I appeal to the United Nations experts in Australia to follow up and render immediate assistance on this matter and interested parties can contact me at mravilaw@gmail.com. This is to ensure that all avenues are exhausted, including the UN mechanism.

16. From the experience of the two cases that I handled pro-bono and where I was only instructed at the clemency stage, hanging takes place within three weeks from the date of the rejection of the clemency on the 3rd Friday. Here we are looking at 11th November 2005.

Breach of Article 9 of the Singapore Constitution – no one shall be deprived of his life save in accordance with law. Accordance with law means due process.

17. The President must satisfy that the Constitution is not breached in the spirit of Article 9 above. Unless he does this, the execution is unlawful, unconstitutional, arbitrary, discriminatory and a violation of the Constitution. Therefore, it is unsafe at this moment to proceed with the execution.

Legal avenues open to Van - The Australian Challenge

18. In the Court of Appeal, Van's lawyers challenged the legality of the mandatory sentence of death, inter alia, on the ground that the death sentence was unconstitutional and therefore illegal. The appellant relied on Articles 9 and 12

An article by Mr.K.S Rajah,SC, former judicial commissioner (annexed herewith)

"The potential use of international law to infuse meaning into domestic law on punishment that is rigid, cruel, inhuman or degrading to make it more flexible and human by the court's exercising discretionary powers when the mandatory sentence is prescribed is now an arguable case."

19. Dealing with the specific mode of execution as being contrary to the prohibition in customary international law against cruel and inhuman treatment in Article 5 of the UDHR which provides:

"No one shall be subjected to torture or to cruel, inhuman or degrading treatment or punishment"

The Court said: "To succeed on this ground of appeal, the appellant must first show that the prohibition against cruel and inhuman treatment or punishment amounts to a customary international rule. Next, the appellant must show that a specific prohibition against hanging as a mode of execution is part of the content of that rule in customary international law."

20. Singapore cannot for long be a global city and player in the world's affairs in every respect - except when it comes to punishing offenders for wrongs done.

It is now open to an accused to show through experts in international law that a mandatory death sentence is cruel and inhuman punishment under customary international law. There is light on the path.

Whether an innocent man can be hanged in Singapore because of Procedure?

21. If as counsel for a condemned person, I am able to adduce fresh evidence or canvass a new argument which has merits, in both situations, after the Appel-

late process has been exhausted (that is, after an appeal has been heard by the Court of Appeal), what recourse does my client, the condemned man, have?

22. As it stands, the court restated their position in the case of Vignes Moorthy v PP that it does not have the power to re-open a case where an appeal had already been heard and dismissed by the Court of Appeal.

23. This is what the Chief Justice meant when he said when Mr Ravi asked the CJ if the public prosecutor was "still maintaining that an innocent man be hanged because of procedure", the CJ answered, "Yes, the answer is yes."

Was Vignes Mourthy innocent? Was he hanged due to the legal procedures in Singapore?

Today Online dated 27September 2003
by Teo Hwee Mak and Joy Frances

24. The aforesaid clearly shows that there is a serious defect in our legal system, since it has undeniably been stated by the Chief Justice himself that an innocent man can be hanged.

25. From my point of view, the courts have revisionary powers which they ought to have defined in Vignes Moorthy's case. Unfortunately, they made a decision which completely shuts the door on the condemned prisoner. This is brutal where an innocent person is concerned because a man is presumed to be innocent.

Article 9 (1) states :

"No person shall be deprived of his life or personal liberty save in accordance with law."

26. Law here means the due process. Due process must mean that an innocent man cannot be hanged.

Further, and in the alternative, the execution of Van should be stayed because it is unsafe to carry out the execution of the applicant as it contravenes Article 9(1) of the Constitution.

27. Putting aside the court system in Singapore, where do we go from here?

"The judges said their court was not the constitutional court therefore could not decide the matter".

Today Online dated 27September 2003
by Teo Hwee Mak and Joy Frances

The problem in relation to the administration of justice in Singapore has to be addressed before a man's life is gone.

Campaign against execution of Van

28. I am appealing to the civil society in Singapore to participate in the upcoming campaign in the next two weeks, details of which will be revealed

shortly in the next couple of days. I have faith that Singaporeans will show their full support regardless of the nationality,religion and ethnic background of anyone who faces imminent execution here. I have faith that Singaporeans will rise above nationality,race and religion in appealing to the President to reconsider his decision.

29. A letter-writing campaign is ongoing as it might help Van to receive letters telling him that Singaporeans care about his situation.

A group of concerned Singaporeans are meeting on Saturday, 7pm at Empires's Café, Raffles Hotel to discuss responses.

Launch of book "Hung At Dawn"

30. On 10th December 2005, I'm releasing a novel on the struggles of two condemned prisoners after their appeals were dismissed. I was involved at the clemency stage in both of these cases, pro bono, when all avenues were closed. There were similar issues raised by me, similarly asking the President to convene the Constitutional Court, which the President turned down without giving any explanation. This book would also form part of the campaign materials for our continued struggle against the death penalty in Singapore.

Dated this 27th Day of October 2005 @ Hotel Grand Plaza, 3 p.m.

M.Ravi

Singapore

Appendix IV

PETITION TO PRESIDENT NOT TO EXECUTE NGUYEN

The Honourable Excellency

The Elected President

Republic of Singapore

c/o Istana Singapore

Office of the Elected President of the Republic of Singapore

Orchard Road

Singapore 238823

27th October 2005

Dear Sir,

REQUEST TO CONVENE A CONSTITUTION TRIBUNAL UNDER ARTICLE 100 OF THE CONSTITUTION OF SINGAPORE NGUYEN TUONG VAN – CONDEMNED PRISIONER NO. 856

It is noted with regret that the Honourable Elected President had turned down the petition for clemency for the above-mentioned Australian citizen. As a private citizen of Singapore, I humbly appeal and urge Your Excellency to accede to my request to convene a Constitutional Tribunal under Article 100 of the Constitution on an urgent basis. This request is made in view of contravention of Articles 9 and 12 of the Constitution and the breach of the principle of natural justice under Article 22(p) of the said Constitution.

This letter is written under the locus standi of a private, concerned Singapore citizen. Your Excellency's order for a Constitutional Tribunal to be convened would be greatly appreciated.

The grounds for the Constitutional Tribunal to be convened are set out in the press release and annexed herewith :

    a) To satisfy that the due process is complied with;

    b) That there is a contravention of the Articles of the Constitution as mentioned above;

    c) That the condemned prisoner had been unfairly and prejudicially treated compared to a British national (Mc Crea) who was extradited to Singapore from Australia and suffers discrimination before our Constitution;

    d) The clemency petition be reconsidered.

As the matter is of great urgency, I would be obliged if Your Excellency would reply by Monday, 31st October 2005.

Yours faithfully,

M. Ravi

ISTANA
SINGAI

Istana Cf 09/01/427

TEL : 68355314
FAX : 67353135

2 November 2005

Mr M Ravi
101 Upper Cross Street
#06-13 People's Park Centre
Singapore 058357

Dear Sir

REQUEST TO APPOINT CONSTITUTIONAL TRIBUNAL
RE: NGUYEN TUONG VAN

Please refer to your letter dated 27 October 2005.

I am directed to inform you that the President, after due consideration, is unable to accede to your request.

Yours sincerely

MRS DORIS TAN-POR
ASST PRINCIPAL PRIVATE SECRETARY
for PRINCIPAL PRIVATE SECRETARY
TO THE PRESIDENT

DEATH PENALTY FIGHT TAKEN TO UN

M. R A V I

---

20 Havelock Raod # 02– 1 0 Central Square S i n g a p o r e 0 5 9765

T e l 6 5 – 6 4288370 F a x : 64288371 E – m a i l : mravilaw@gmail.com

www.mravilaw.com

D a t e : 7th November 2005

Mr. Philip Alston

United Nations Special Rapporteur on Extrajudicial ,

Summary or Arbitrary Executions

c/o OHCHR-UNOG,1211 Geneva 10, Switzerland

By Fax : (+41 22)9179006) & email

Dear Mr.Philip Alston,

IMMINENT EXECUTION OF NGUYEN TUONG VAN-25YRS OLD (AUSTRALIAN) IN SINGAPORE - URGENT APPEAL FOR UN INTERVENTION TO STAVE OFF THE EXECUTION SCHEDULED ON 11TH OR 18TH NOVEMBER 2005 INDIVIDUAL COMPLAINT FROM SINGAPORE

I refer to the above matter.

Introduction

I am a human rights lawyer from Singapore who was involved in the recent anti-death penalty campaign in Singapore in the case of Shanmugam Murugesu v PP where a similar complaint like this one was lodged to your good office. At that time I was also Shanmugam's lawyer.

I am very pleased to read a report from www.theage.com.au in which you have stated that Australia ought to pursue the issue in Nguyen's case that mandatory death penalty in drug cases contravened international Law.

The Australian Government had claimed that due process had been complied with in Nguyen's case.

Therefore, the only avenue they seem to have looked at was the diplomatic channel, which has now come to a dead end and the Singapore State is proceeding to execute Nguyen either this Friday 11th November 2005 or on 18th November 2005 (execution usually takes place on the 3rd week upon the rejection of the clemency petition).

I held a press conference on 26th October 2005 with the local and Australian media, as well as with the Australian and British High Commissions. Through this press conference, I endeavoured to highlight that due process had not been complied with in so far as the Clemency process is concerned. I also highlighted other avenues open to Nguyen. I enclose herewith a copy of my press release which contains my detailed arguments . I wish to highlight the salient points for your due consideration in my complaint to your good office against the Singapore and the Australian governments and look to the United Nations for an urgent intervention on the matters raised below.

Due process of Law had not been complied during the clemency process involving Nguyen's Clemency Plea

There are two violations of the Constitution of Singapore in relation to the Clemency process :

1. Article 12 of the Singapore Constitution that guarantees equality and equal treatment before the law had been contravened because Nguyen had been prejudicially treated on the issue of clemency as compared to Mc Crea (a British national)

Discrimination before the Singapore Constitution

Singapore government gave an undertaking to the Australian government that Mc Crea would not be executed in the event that he is extradited to Singapore and convicted of double murder in Singapore. Basically, even before Mc Crea's trial had begun, the Singapore Executive had exercised their discretion to grant clemency to Mc Crea, a British national who was arrested in Australia for the double murders in Singapore.

Mc Crea was extradited from Australia just around the same time when Nguyen's clemency was turned down after diplomatic means had failed to convince the Singapore government not to proceed with the execution of Nguyen. The judges have been denied by Singapore laws as interpreted by the judiciary that they do not have discretion in mandatory death sentence. However, executive discretion had been applied in a discriminatory manner in Nguyen's case and hence he had been prejudicially treated on his clemency plea.

Discrimination before Australian Constitution

The fact that the Australian government did not secure a clemency for Nguyen vis-à-vis Mc Crea's case smacks of discrimination of Nguyen before the Australian Constitution. It raises the question as to whether Nguyen's Clemency was ever brought into the negotiation process and as to whether it was even suggested as part of a condition by the Australian government to extradite Mc Crea to Singapore. Why no undertaking was given by the Singapore government in Nguyen's case when a similar undertaking not to impose the death penalty was given in Mc Crea's case. This is clearly discriminatory.

2. Clemency/Pardon process spelt out under Article22P of the Singapore Constituition is defective as it breaches the Principles of Natural Justice

Aticle 22P states : Grant of Pardon

".......after the Attorney- General has given his opinion thereon, the reports shall be sent, together with the Attorney-General's opinion, to the Cabinet so that the Cabinet may advise the President on the exercise of the power conferred on him.."

It is crystal clear that there has been a clear conflict and a breach of the principles of Natural Justice for the Attorney-General, who prosecuted the condemned prisoner, to render an opinion in advising the Cabinet on the issue of clemency. Similar Constitutional challenges of this nature on the clemency process had been successfully mounted in some Commonwealth countries. The Attorney-General's major involvement in the Clemency process has made the quality of mercy so strained.

By reason of the aforesaid breaches of the Constitution, I had in my capacity as a citizen petitioned the President at the press conference held on 26th October in urging His Excellency to convene a Constitutional Tribunal under Article 100 to investigate whether there had been violations of due process since article 9 says no one shall be deprived of his life save in accordance with law. Law here means due process must be complied with.

The President replied yesterday by way of his Excellency's letter dated 2nd November 2005 which stated that the President is unable to accede to my request to convene a Constitutional Tribunal.

Complaint against the Singapore Government to UN Special Rapporteur on Extra-judicial,summary,or arbitrary executions

Since the President has declined to convene a constitutional tribunal, I am now placing a complaint against the Singapore Government with your good office to investigate the violation of the due process under the United Nations Declaration of Human Rights and the various breaches stated above as outlined in my press release attached to this document.

Complaint against the Australian Government to UN Special Rapporteur on Extra-judicial,summary,or arbitrary executions

I wish to also place a complaint against the Australian government before your good office on the failure of the Australian government to ensure that due process was complied with as Nguyen suffers discrimination and prejudicial treatment in contravention of the Australian Constitution .

Even if the Australian Government continues to adopt the view that due process had been followed, in the interest of Nguyen they ought to take the matter to the International Court of Justice ("ICJ"). This is based on the arguments put forward by Nguyen's lawyers that **mandatory death sentence** (especially for drug-related offences) **is cruel and inhuman punishment under international law** and the same arguments can be canvassed before the ICJ. This is provided that the Prime Minister of Australia is still keen to explore any opportunity to save Nguyen from being executed. Since Mr. Philip

Aliston is appraised of all these issues, the Australian government could see his immediate valuable guidance in the matter.

I wish to also place on record that I am filing a second complaint against the Australian government to the UN Rapporteur for extra-judicial and summary, arbitrary executions in the event that the Australian government fails to refer the matter to ICJ by 10.00am on Wednesday 9th November 2005. Time lines are important as deadlines are closing and I do not intend any impudence in this regard. Other governments opposed to the death penalty, such as Germany in LeGrand's case, had brought such matters to the ICJ before on the issue of due process claiming this had /.not been complied with by the US government, as well numerous cases pending before the ICJ.

The purpose of referring matters before ICJ to a third party is to foster the diplomatic relations rather than the governments having to risk diplomatic ties. This ICJ route is in favour of Australia and Singapore as well. Singapore's government can stave off the execution pending the outcome of ICJ's decision. ICJ can equally make an order to stave off the execution of Nguyen.

In the circumstances, I humbly urge your good office to urgently intervene in stopping this man-made disaster from taking place. You may also reach me on my mobile if you require any clarification.

Yours sincerely

M.Ravi

the REACH OUT campaign

We are Kelly and Bronwyn, close friends of Van. We have visited him on death row in Singapore on numerous occasions. Van is like a brother to Kelly, a best friend to Bronwyn. This is our personal plea to ask you to Reach Out and help save Van's life.

This campaign stems from a genuine and true relationship between Van and his mother, Kim. The last time she visited Van, Van reached out to his mother, placed his hand on the glass trying to Reach Out to her and said, *"You hold my hand,"* and Kim replied, *"I hold you forever."* Kim placed her hand to meet his on the other side of the glass. She relives that moment with tears everyday. Despite travelling many miles to be close to him, friends and family are still separated by the glass. Smeared with fingerprints, the glass that divides us becomes a barrier to an integral part of kinship and friendship– human touch.

Upon each visit, Van instinctively puts his hand on the glass to Reach Out to try to touch us. We naturally put our hands on the other side of the glass to meet his.

When we visit we sit as close to the glass as possible. In one letter he told us *"Our last visit... We were so close....It was unfortunate you weren't able to sit against the glass longer. But one second was enough to last forever in our memories."*

Van has fully admitted his guilt. He has expressed clearly that he accepts responsibility for his actions and is completely remorseful for his wrongdoing. Even as close friends, we know that his offence requires imprisonment. However, not execution. His assistance to the Australian Federal Police since his imprisonment is important because all sensible justice systems give lower level prisoners a lesser sentence if they help authorities against more senior criminals. The laws of Singapore and Australia allow for this. However we believe that his assistance, deep sorrow and remorse have gone unnoticed in Singapore.

Van has spent the last three years not knowing if his life will end at the end of a rope. The Singapore government believes our friend should be punished by death, declaring that they will not forgive someone who has repented. This is a case where the penalty far outweighs the crime, and ignores the conduct after the crime - that is, his help to the police. We are not asking for special treatment. The Constitution allows for a lesser penalty in these circumstances.

In one of his letters to us, Van wrote about his friend who was about to be executed in the next few days, *"It breaks my heart because there is only so much I can do for him. My priority will be him and making sure he'll have all the support he can get."*

For a young man whose greatest strength now is that he never fails to Reach Out to others in need, he does not deserve to die. The President of Singapore has the power to save Van's life.

By tracing your hand, you will be making a direct request to the President to spare Van's life. If spared, Van would spend most of his adult years in prison, however he will have life and continue to share the love he gives and receives. Trace your hand on coloured paper and write your message of support to Van inside your hand – we will display them all in a public mural. Your hand will Reach Out and carry your support directly to the President. In life we learn and we all make mistakes. Please find the mercy and humanity to help us to save our brother, our dear friend. Please Reach Out now to help us save Van.

Send your hand to: Kelly Ng and Bronwyn Lew
                      The Reach Out Campaign
                      c/o Howells, 205 William St, Melbourne 3000, Australia

You are also like my son. My son has told me about you before he died. Shanmugam told me to save you even if he is to die.

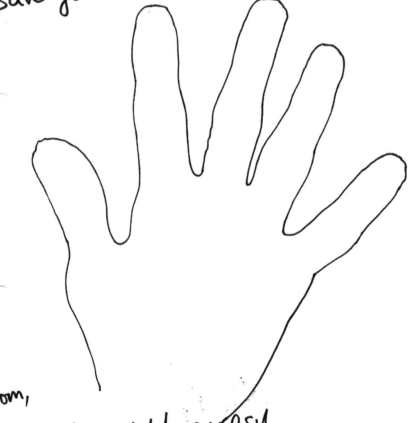

From,

Mdm Letchumi Murugesu
mother of Shanmugam Murugesu
7/11/2005

Sunday 30th October 2005

To the Murugesu Family and Mr M. Ravi,

My name is Kelly Ng and I am an old high school friend of Van Nguyen's. Van is like a little brother to me and I love him dearly. I have visited Van in Singapore four times since his imprisonment.

There was a newspaper article printed in a Melbourne newspaper on Friday October 2005, about you conveying what Shanmugam had said about Van. I am writing to express my gratitude and appreciation for speaking out. It really means a lot to me. Upon reading the article, I could not help but shed a few tears. Van's family, friends and lawyers are incredibly touched and it has given us much comfort as well as encouragement to keep fighting.

I am very sorry for your loss and I share your pain. I hope that our courage to stand up for what we believe in will one day abolish the death penalty in Singapore so that other families will not have experience what we are going through.

I do not know how else to express my gratitude. Know that you will always be in my prayers. Thankyou!

Best regards,

Kelly Ng

SHANMUGAM s/o MURUGESU

Hanged 13 May 2005

His friends called him Sam. National Jet ski champion. Beloved son. Father of twin boys. Accused of peddling marijuana. His impoverished, abandoned family will never recover.

HOW LONG WILL WE LET THIS CARRY ON?

NGUYEN TUONG VAN

To hang Nov 2005

No previous criminal record. Born in a refugee camp in Thailand, moved to Australia with his mother and twin brother when he was 6 months old. Agreed to carry a packet of heroin in order to pay off his twin brother's debts. First trip outside Australia.

ABOLISH THE DEATH PENALTY IN SINGAPORE & EVERYWHERE!

BECAUSE it doesn't reduce crime rates | BECAUSE it doesn't deter criminals | BECAUSE it doesn't make societies safer or more humane | BECAUSE a majority of developed societies have already banned it — and are better off; safer and more peaceful without it | BECAUSE it is overridingly and arbitrarily used against the poorest, least educated peoples on our planet | BECAUSE public outrage of crime can be channeled more positively and productively | BECAUSE it doesn't bring closure but opens new wounds | BECAUSE it doesn't even necessarily save money! | BECAUSE there is no fail safe judiciary in the world | BECAUSE we continue to get it wrong!

This is a scaled image of the actual tracing of Van's hand which he sent in a letter to his mother, and which has been used in the Reach Out campaign initiated by his friends Kelly Ng and Bronwyn Lew. You can send hands of support to:

The Reach Out Campaign c/o Howells, 205 William Street, Melbourne 3000, or directly to Van at the addresses listed inside this flyer.

UNITED NATIONS

Press Release

EXPERT ON ARBITRARY EXECUTIONS CALLS ON SINGAPORE
GOVERNMENT NOT TO CARRY OUT MANDATORY DEATH SENTENCE
15 November 2005

The Special Rapporteur on extrajudicial, summary or arbitrary executions of the United Nations Commission on Human Rights issued the following statement today:

Philip Alston, the Special Rapporteur on extrajudicial, summary or arbitrary executions of the United Nations Commission on Human Rights, today called on the Government of Singapore not to proceed with the planned execution of Nguyen Tuong Van. Mr Nguyen was sentenced to death for attempting to traffic just under 400 grams of pure heroin through Changi Airport in December 2002.

Mr. Alston, a law professor at New York University, said that the execution of Mr Nguyen would violate international legal standards relating to the imposition of the death penalty.

The principal problem, according to Alston, is the mandatory nature of the death penalty. "Making such a penalty mandatory – thereby eliminating the discretion of the court – makes it impossible to take into account mitigating or extenuating circumstances and eliminates any individual determination of an appropriate sentence in a particular case", Alston noted. "The adoption of such a black-and-white approach is entirely inappropriate where the life of the accused is at stake. Once the sentence has been carried out, it is irreversible."

In the Nguyen case, the Singapore Court of Appeal considered a range of cases decided by the Privy Council. But, according to Alston, "it failed to examine the most relevant case of all"

(Boyce and Joseph v. The Queen, decided in 2004). In that case, four of the Law Lords endorsed the statement that "No international human rights tribunal anywhere in the world has ever found a mandatory death penalty regime compatible with international human rights norms."

Professor Alston noted that the Singaporean Government had, in the past, stated that "the death penalty is primarily a question for the sovereign jurisdiction of each country". He indicated, however, that matters relating to the functioning of the criminal justice system are legitimate matters of international concern when questions of non-compliance with international standards are involved.

Noting the longstanding commitment of the Singaporean courts to the rule of law, Alston called upon the Government of Singapore to take all necessary steps to avoid an execution which is inconsistent with accepted standards of international human rights law.

ABOLISH THE DEATH PENALTY IN SINGAPORE & EVERYWHERE!

BECAUSE IT DOESN'T LOWER CRIME

BECAUSE IT DOESN'T DETER CRIMINALS

BECAUSE IT DOESN'T MAKE SOCIETIES ANY SAFER OR MORE HUMANE

BECAUSE A MAJORITY OF DEVELOPED SOCIETIES ARE ALREADY
SAFER AND MORE PEACEFUL WITHOUT IT

BECAUSE IT IS OVERWHELMINGLY AND ARBITRARILY USED AGAINST
THE POOREST, LEAST EDUCATED PEOPLES ON OUR PLANET

BECAUSE PUBLIC OUTRAGE AT CRIME CAN BE USED
MORE PRODUCTIVELY

BECAUSE IT DOESN'T EVEN SAVE MONEY!

BECAUSE IT DOESN'T BRING CLOSURE, BUT OPENS NEW WOUNDS

BECAUSE THERE IS NO FAIL-SAFE JUDICIARY IN THE WORLD

BECAUSE WE CONTINUE TO GET IT WRONG.

ABOLISH THE DEATH PENALTY IN SINGAPORE & EVERYWHERE.

DEATH PENALTY INFORMATION CENTRE USA

www.deathpenaltyinfo.org

AUSTRALIAN COALITION AGAINST DEATH PENALTY

www.acadp.org

AMNESTY INTERNATIONAL

www.amnesty.org

THINK CENTRE SINGAPORE

www.thinkcentre.org

SINGAPORE DEMOCRATIC PARTY

www.singaporedemocrat.org

www.vallalar.org

www.stophanging.com

www.hungatdawn.blogspot.com